THE HUMILIATION OF THE CHURCH

THE HUMILIATION
OF
THE CHURCH

by

Albert H. van den Heuvel

THE WESTMINSTER PRESS

Philadelphia

LIBRARY OF CONGRESS CATALOG CARD NO. 66–20095

Published by The Westminster Press ®
Philadelphia, Pennsylvania

PRINTED IN THE UNITED STATES OF AMERICA

CONTENTS

FOREWORD

THE FOLLOWING ESSAYS and speeches cover a period of five years' work in the Youth Department of the World Council of Churches. They represent sixty months of trying to interpret the anger and disillusionment of a younger generation to the leaders of our denominations, and to communicate the excitement of what has been said and done to bring about the renewal of the life of the church. I hope they will be read as such.

In a few years' time, I am sure we shall all smile about what is said (and sometimes shouted) in the following pages. History moves quickly, and we change within it. We all now need to start building again. The movement of protest is old enough to start the work of reconstruction.

The notes in this book are an invitation to read further on the subject rather than to give it a more academic appearance. For the same reason, the non-English literature is given priority.

Valerie Tong, as usual, interrupted, completed, ordered, and guided my efforts on the following topics.

ALBERT H. VAN DEN HEUVEL

I

SECULARIZATION
AS FREEDOM AND YOKE

"I BEGAN by saying that God is being increasingly edged out of the world, now that it has come of age. Knowledge and life are thought to be perfectly possible without him. . . . Theology has endeavoured to produce an apologetic to meet this development, engaging in futile rearguard actions against Darwinism, etc. At other times it has accommodated itself to this development by restricting God to the so-called last questions as a kind of *Deus ex machina*. God thus became the answer to life's problems, the solution of its distresses and conflicts. As a result, if anyone had no such difficulties, if he refused to identify himself in sympathy with those who had, it was no good trying to win him for God. . . . If a man won't see that his happiness is really damnation, his health sickness, his vigour and vitality despair; if he won't call them what they really are, the theologian is at his wits' end. He must be a hardened sinner of a particularly vicious type. If not, he is a case of bourgeois complacency, and the one is as far from salvation as the other. . . .

"When God was driven out of the world, and from the public side of human life, an attempt was made to retain him at least in the sphere of the 'personal,' the 'inner life,' the private life. And since every man still has a private sphere, it was thought that he was most vulnerable at this point. . . .

"This is why I am so anxious that God should not be relegated to some last secret place, but that we should frankly recognize that the world and men have come of age, that we should not speak ill of man in his worldliness, but confront him with God at his strongest point. . . .

"And the only way to be honest is to recognize that we have to live in the world *etsi deus non daretur* [as if God did not exist]. And this is just what we do see—before God! So our coming of age forces us to a true recognition of our situation *vis à vis* God. God is teaching us that we must live as men who can get along very well without him. The God who is with us is the God who forsakes us (Mark 15:34). The God who makes us live in this world without using him as a working hypothesis is the God before whom we are ever standing. Before God and with him we live without God. God allows himself to be edged out of the world and on to the cross. God is weak and powerless in the world, and that is exactly the way, the only way, in which he can be with us and help us. Matthew 8:17 makes it crystal clear that it is not by his omnipotence that Christ helps us, but by his weakness and suffering.

"This is the decisive difference between Christianity and all religions. Man's religiosity makes him look in his distress to the power of God in the world; he uses God as a *Deus ex machina*. The Bible however directs him to the powerlessness and suffering of God; only a suffering God can help. To this extent we may say that the process we have described by which the world came of age was an abandonment of a false conception of God, and a clearing of the decks for the God of the Bible, who conquers power and space in the world by his weakness."[1]

It is now twenty years since Dietrich Bonhoeffer was executed by his own countrymen as a traitor to the national cause. These somewhat lengthy quotations are from three letters that were written from prison not long before that ominous date. Ever since then, these lines, which I have once again called to your memory, have caused liberation, discussion, and fury in the Christian world. Bonhoeffer was not the first to dedicate much of his thinking to the process of secularization, but he was one of the first Christians to evaluate it positively.

Until the Second World War, secularization was a spook in Western Europe, the henchman of the Antichrist who emptied the churches and made laymen in the church stand up against their priests and ministers, or who even killed the faith in millions of people. Secularization was the program of the Communists who actively fought the church, the body of Christ, took away her goods, forbade her to teach the nation what was good and bad, and successfully taught that religion was an opiate which enslaved people so that they did not resist exploitation and tutelage but were passively waiting for heaven, where they would be rewarded for their long-suffering patience and faith.

Secularization meant empty churches, no vocations for theological studies, fewer and fewer baptisms and confirmations. It meant that the church was edged out of the world and (in the understanding of many) that God, living in the church, was therefore doomed to become a refugee. The faithful were therefore called to the barricades to defend church and God against these men of darkness who felt strong enough to live without God and whose independence had already penetrated into politics and culture.[2]

Then there came this Lutheran theologian from Germany who had always been an independent spirit and whose strongly confessional early writings had gradually changed into a theology of flexibility. This carried him through an almost monastic period, a pacifist period, into the last years of his life as an active underground fighter against Hitler. Bonhoeffer, as we have seen from a few quotations, speaks about secularization as a liberation: *"an abandonment of a false conception of God, and the clear-*

ing of the decks for the God of the Bible." That idea was new for most of us. This description of the process of secularization without the immediate anathema of the churchly reaction opened our eyes to a whole new field of study. Bonhoeffer seemed to be quite happy with the thing we were always warned against, and he was clearly no atheist. On the contrary, the reader of his earlier books *The Cost of Discipleship* and *Life Together* gets the impression of a highly committed, almost absolutist, orthodox theologian whose use of the Bible was not very critical and sometimes rather naïve. Walter Harrelson says, "We may not have learned from him too much about the task and method of full-scale exegetical work on the Bible . . . [but] he could teach us to learn and to live and to die with the Biblical word in our hands; should we ask for more?"[3]

It seems that Bonhoeffer's radical acceptance of secularization does not at all rule out a life that is lived in a secret discipline of prayer and meditation, of study, worship, and silence. Behind these two elements in his works is the unshaken certitude that faith is an initiative which comes from the other side to us, with its own inescapable and undeniable reality. Our conceptualization of that faith, our beliefs and convictions, our confessions and dogmas, our understanding, and our ability to systematize our belief may have suffered and may even have become impossible, but faith is a gift and as such cannot be destroyed except by Him who gave it in the first place. In faith, as in love, there is no fear, because in faith, as in love, there is perfect freedom, which allows us to think and to study the reality in which we live with full integrity, honesty, and—again—freedom.

That was the legacy which a whole generation of Christians—theologians and laymen—received from the martyr of Flossenbürg.

What has the church done with it? That question cannot be answered easily. I think it is fair to say that no theologian, including the great church father of Basel, has had such an influence on the younger theologians as has Bonhoeffer. His last thoughts were only sketchy and unfinished, and some of his key concepts, such as "a world come of age," "arcana-discipline," and "religionless Christianity," have been very differently explained and often rightly criticized, but even so, the main challenge from these few letters written in prison has captured many theologians. But the church as such could not do much with it. Our institutions are by far too religious to be able to digest such scathing criticism of metaphysics and individualism, and our faith is by far too institutionalized to understand Bonhoeffer's plea for a church that would pay its own ministers and would meet when it suited us rather than on the sacrosanct Sunday. There has been no synod that canonized Bonhoeffer's theology, and his description of Christians as "simply men, who stand by God in his hour of grieving" has not been really digested. His insistence on the powerlessness of God in this world and his insights into Christianity as the only community—over against all religions—which does not call God to help them out but which, rather, participates in Jesus' everlasting suffering (cf. Rev., ch. 5, and Pascal!) is still a foreign idea in much of our theologizing.

But this strange theology of the weakness of God has penetrated into many a study and activity. And we should like to look a bit at that.

The Understanding of the Process of Secularization

Since the Second World War, and with the initial push from Dietrich Bonhoeffer, the reflection on the process of secularization has been much deepened, especially from the Christian point of view. Once it was discovered that this whole process was not half so dangerous as people had believed, theologians started to study it rather thoroughly. One of the most impressive studies comes from Friedrich Gogarten in his *Verhängnis und Hoffnung der Neuzeit, die Säkularisierung als theologisches Problem,* in which he gives as a definition of secularization that it is the *"Vergeschichtlichung der menschlichen Existenz"* (the historization of the human existence), the notion which modern man has much more strongly than ever before that he is a historical being, a person with an end and a beginning; that he is not just part of a cycle, but that he comes from somewhere and goes somewhere else. He is there once and for all, and if he wants to produce something, he has to do it here and now.

We meet here the *historical* interpretation of secularization, which is very important for its meaning. Not only is secularization the process by which man becomes aware of his own historicity, but the process has started in a definite period of history and is not something that is with us, like fashion, which may disappear again tomorrow. Secularization in Western Europe started way back before the Reformation and has been among us ever since, always gathering momentum, always becoming closer to the people, always eating away at the authority of the church.

To quote Bonhoeffer again: "On the historical side I should say there is *one* great development which leads to the idea of the autonomy of the world. In theology it is first discernible in Lord Herbert of Cherbury, with his assertion that reason is the sufficient instrument of religious knowledge. In ethics it first appears in Montaigne and Bodin with their substitution of moral principles for the ten commandments. In politics, Machiavelli, who emancipates politics from the tutelage of morality, and founds the doctrine of 'reasons of state.' Later, and very differently, though like Machiavelli tending towards the autonomy of human society, comes Grotius, with his international law as the law of nature, a law which would still be valid, *etsi deus non daretur*. The process is completed in philosophy. On the one hand we have the deism of Descartes, who holds that the world is a mechanism which runs on its own without any intervention of God. On the other hand there is the pantheism of Spinoza, with its identification of God with nature. In the last resort Kant is a deist, Fichte and Hegel pantheists. All along the line there is a growing tendency to assert the autonomy of man and the world.

"In natural science the process seems to start with Nicolas of Cusa and Giordano Bruno with their 'heretical' doctrine of the infinity of space. The classical cosmos was finite, like the created world of the Middle Ages. An infinite universe, however it be conceived, is self-subsisting *etsi deus non daretur*. . . .

"There is no longer any need for God as a working hypothesis, whether in morals, politics or science. Nor is there any need for such a God in religion or philosophy (Feuerbach)."[4]

In the historical interpretation of secularization, there are two related developments emphasized from the beginning. One is the process by which man is liberated gradually from the control of metaphysics and theology. That does not mean that modern man necessarily denies a metaphysical reality, it only means that, whatever these realities are, they do not *control* man any longer. The church as the most important "metaphysical agent" in European society gradually lost control over human activities and thought patterns. At the beginning of the Middle Ages, the church and its theology controlled the whole of life—politics, economics, law, education, medicine, morals, even eternal life. Today all those human activities are independent. Theology may be an important partner in the discussion (it may also be a very unimportant partner!), but it no longer *controls* any of the subjects. The other side of the coin here is that man in this process becomes more and more independent; he is "coming of age." He may pay lip service to God as the necessary power behind all that takes place, but he has taken his own fate into his own hands. Only small groups of people refuse modern medicine or democracy or state schools. All of us now put our fate into the hands of the engineers, politicians, doctors, and scientists, and we do so quite happily.

The other side of the picture is that in this process God lost more and more of his original attributes. The study of space made him homeless (heaven is not to be located). The study of biology revealed that he did not manufacture man in seven days, but that there was a long process of evolution through which man developed out of the unicellular entities of millions of years ago. The study of history showed that the Bible is a human book and has a history interwoven with the history of the times of its origin, and therefore cannot be infallible—God is not its author. The history of science shows that man can do almost anything without ever meeting God. Today we are about to discover how to make life, and we shall undoubtedly succeed. The study of psychology finally showed that even the dark rooms of the inner self are the abode of lusts and instincts rather than the abode of God.

After the historical interpretation of secularization, which shows that perhaps the stage at which we are is not final but that the process as such is undoubtedly irreversible, there is the sociological interpretation of the development.[5] The sociologist sees secularization simply as a result of differentiation, which is also a historical process by which man keeps on top of a very complex society. In order to come to grips with the rapidly changing and ever flexible problems of a mobile society, we have differentiated its institutions (social, political, economic, and cultural) more and more. We have experts and detailed studies. We have people with differentiated responsibilities. The old static structure with a strict hierarchy and social institutions to which all belonged, the time of the scholar who knew all there was to know, belongs definitely to the past.

The sociologist says that what happened to the church was simply that, in a differentiated society, the church lost its oversight and its central place. In a process of ongoing differentiation, that was simply unavoidable. The church is now responsible for religion and nothing else! (The sociological amateur says: The church is the place where people spend their Sundays only; it has no relevance to the other activities of the week!) Harvey Cox in his *The Secular City*[6] points to urbanization as almost the twin sister of secularization. He celebrates the city as the fatherland and promised land for the secular man and sees secularization as the most important tool to bring about the modern metropolis. Cox is writing mainly about city life, and as such his use of the process of secularization is enlightening. As long as nobody thinks that the village, the town, and the smaller city can escape this rolling tank, no harm is done, but we should not limit the influence of secularization to its urban form.

Most fascinating is the *Biblical* interpretation of secularization. Dr. A. van Leeuwen in his *Christianity in World History* makes this quite plain. "This takes its beginning in Israel," he says. "Here is raised the protest against the reality of the cosmic totality, against the 'sacralizing' of all being, against the supremacy of fate, against the divinizing of kings and kingdoms. Here a break is made with the everlasting cycle of nature and the timeless presentness of myth. Here history is discovered, where the covenant between the Creator and the creation, between the Lord and his people, bursts open the solid oneness of the universe. Here there is proper room for man and here is the taste of freedom. The world is now radically secularized, becomes creation moving forward to regeneration, is made the arena of history, is in much pain and travail, waiting for the redemption and consummation of all things. . . . In the course of history the nation which had raised the sword of secularization against its enemies finds that same weapon directed against itself. It is within Israel that the sacred kingship is destroyed, the holy temple brought down and the holy people scattered among the nations. In the New Testament this history reaches its climax at the cross of Golgotha where God's judgement is passed upon the Messiah of Israel, upon God's own appointed Son."[7]

The Biblical interpretation of secularization—which finds powerful defenders in men like Gogarten, Bonhoeffer, Winter, Cox—states clearly that the process started with the call to Israel by that nameless God of Abraham and Moses, in which man was freed from invisible control and put in charge of the whole inhabited earth. In the Bible there is nothing sacred but God himself, and on this earth man is put in charge. As the author of Ps. 115 sings: "The heavens are the Lord's heavens, but the earth he has given to the sons of men" (v. 16). One should read again some of the parables of Jesus, where the world is called a vineyard given to his servants to look after, or where the servants are given talents to work with in freedom. Here there are no taboos on science or limitations to the human enterprise. On the contrary, man is God's collaborator in overpowering the powers and subduing the earth.

Dr. Berkhof says: "Many, Christians as well as non-Christians, believe that this process of Christianization stopped in the periods of the Renaissance and the Enlightenment and was gradually replaced by a basically different process—that of secularization. This is a false opinion, however. Secularization is, in the first place, the continuation of Christianization. The difference lies in the fact that in modern times the consequences of the gospel are mainly drawn by those who are outside of the church and who are not aware of the source of their inspiration. These times are characterized by the discoveries of *science* and the inventions of *techniques*. . . . Without this radical change in man's concept of nature [because in Israel man understood God to be on his side against nature], science, techniques, fight against diseases, etc., never would have taken place [in Europe and North America] to the extent to which they have.

"The consequences of secularism in *social and political areas* also have a Christian background. The gospel introduced a God who is not another name for the existing social order, but a revolutionary God, whose 'righteousness' (*sedek*), according to the Psalms and the prophets, means that he lifts up those who are bowed down and humiliates the oppressors. . . . This new image of social standards is the primary source of our modern *revolutions,* in which again and again new groups of oppressed claim their rights. The French Revolution, with its ideals of liberty, equality, and fraternity, had far more to do with Jesus Christ than had those who resisted it in the name of Christ. . . . The liberating and transforming power of the Spirit of Jesus Christ is at work everywhere where men are freed from the tyranny of nature, state, color, caste, class, sex, poverty, disease, and ignorance."[8]

It should be clear from these last two quotations that a very new dimension of the Christian faith has been discovered. Of course there are many questions here, and they need careful and detailed attention, but a major discovery has been made.

Ecumenical Dimensions

Some people may think that these thoughts are only the hallucinations of a few Protestants who speculate about a possible way out of the devastation of secularization. But this ongoing debate on the true understanding of the secular has *ecumenical dimensions*. The interested reader should try to find the minutes of the third session of the Second Vatican Council and read especially what the Fathers of the Councils have said about the famous Schema 13: *Ecclesia in mundo moderno*. Many of the same trends can be read there. Other Roman Catholics have written and said many of the same things. In the World Council of Churches there is a wealth of material on the subject. The Study on *The Missionary Structure of the Congregation,* for instance, speaks about many of the same realities.[9] The World Student Christian Federation has dedicated an issue of the *Student World* to secularization, in which the articles of Dr. van Peursen warrant special mention.[10]

The European Life and Mission of the Church conference in Graz showed how important this subject is in the life of European Christian students (and how confused!).

It is useful to distinguish carefully between secularization—as the process by which man and society are liberated from the control of metaphysics and theology—and secularism, which is an ideology (in the words of Dr. van Leeuwen) that is fixed and absolutized and that has a tendency toward pagan or nihilistic totalitarianism. The first, secularization, we have described in some detail; the second, secularism, should be understood as that ideology which believes that the process of secularization is the ongoing self-explication of truth, which requires belief from all people. In the process of secularization, metaphysical realities have lost their functionality and are no longer working hypotheses, but secularism denies their existence and becomes a historical materialism, which enslaves man anew. Secularism, therefore, annihilates the fruits of secularization. Dr. C. F. von Weizsäcker has repeatedly pleaded for a humble use of the fruits of secularization and given attention to the ambiguity of the phenomenon.[11]

The Ambiguity of Secularization

In the foregoing I have described secularization in a very positive way, and the literature indicated has one-sidedly given attention to those theologians and lay Christians who have helped to work out the positive aspects of this process.

However, Bonhoeffer has already carefully indicated that although the gospel speaks about secular realities in a secular world, it is easy to fall into the pitfall of speaking about *secularized* realities in a *secularized* world. There is a great difference in these two concepts. We have discovered that the Bible is a secular book, or, in other words, that in it the main interest is in concrete events happening on earth. God revealed himself definitely and fully in Jesus, to whom we give the title Christ for that very reason. We, man, do not come from heaven, nor are we looking forward to eternal life in heaven. We are *earthlings,* born on *earth* of *earthly* fathers and mothers. When we are reborn by God's acceptance of the sacrifice of Christ, which took place on *earth,* we are expecting and hoping for the new *earth.*

That incredible revelation is given to us in the incarnation of Christ in a language, not of heaven, but of the first century A.D. The Messiah did not live cosmically without a fixed habitat, but he lived on earth, in a specific country, under a specific political system, and was a man, clothed in the garments of his time, who spoke the vernacular of his country, and who used no universal method of communication but spoke and taught as a common rabbi of the Pharisee group.

It is this *earthliness* of the incarnation story which makes us say that the gospel is secular. It is concrete and specific. Like the whole community of Israel it was again and again called back by prophets from metaphysical speculations. Its job was to testify to a God who acted concretely in history, and who did not require complicated religious observances but asked for mercy which would show the nations that JHWH himself was merciful and righteous. The return to that secular reality is called by Bonhoeffer the quest for "religionless Christianity," not because it lacks all activities and thoughts that are normally called religious, but because they do not seek the salvation of the individual and because they refrain from calling God to our side as a special privilege. Religionless Christianity for Bonhoeffer is to live like Jesus, i.e., *for others,* in the powerlessness and weakness which characterize the Messianic ministry of Christ.

The secularized man, however, is the one who has fallen for secularism. He *refuses* to pray and proclaims that God is dead. He is no longer an agnostic who only knows little and who only accepts the (secondary) metaphysical aspects of the Gospels because they were dear to his Master, but he has become the faithful slave of a new ideology. He speaks about the secular world—which only means the concrete world—as if it is now without God, forgetting that he can only say that because God himself has told him to live that way. The secularized man lives on the fruits of secularization, pretending that they are his rights.

The ambiguity of secularization also stems from the simple fact that it is a process. When we were freed from the control of metaphysics, we did not necessarily become free men; on the contrary, many people ran to other gods and became even more enslaved to them. Real freedom occurs only when we stay close enough to the Great Secular Man himself and do not fall for other masters.[12]

Let me close with a few words about the ongoing discussion. The fruits of Bonhoeffer's initial contribution are best felt in two realms of the church: its theology and its structures.

In theology there are various discussions going on to implement what Bonhoeffer has opened up. Three discussions seem to me to be most important.

A somewhat confused, but highly interesting, debate surrounds the little book by Bishop J. A. T. Robinson, *Honest to God.*[13] He made an attempt to find the common link between the theological schools of Bultmann, Tillich, and Bonhoeffer, but chose for himself in the end a Tillichian perspective in his thinking. Many people, the Bishop included, would agree that *The Honest to God Debate*[13] was much more revealing and thoroughgoing than the fuse that lighted it. The discussion is mainly concerned with honesty in our conceptualizations of our faith and with the way in which we can express what we believe in terms that make sense to ourselves and to those with whom we speak. In *Honest to God* the practical chapters have played a greater role of liberation for those readers who came to these ideas afresh than do the first chapters which deal with the nature and image of God.

Another fascinating attempt to make sense out of the person of Christ in a secular society comes from Paul van Buren,[14] who was convinced by the so-called language analysts[15] that we have to be infinitely more careful with the language we speak and the concepts we use. Van Buren, who believes that the word "God" no longer makes sense because it has "died the death of a thousand qualifications," sees the whole gospel summed up in the concept of freedom. The book, which is written almost as a personal confession, makes more sense to the Christian than to the non-Christian, probably because it needs the background of a thorough knowledge of the Old Testament and the Biblical content of the word "freedom."

A much fuller attempt—in the sense of treating more aspects of the faith—to speak in nonreligious terms about the gospel is Ebeling's *The Nature of Faith*,[16] in which a strongly Lutheran emphasis on faith is related to a very lucid explanation of historical categories. This book speaks more to non-Christians than to Christians apparently, because many faithful see "nothing new" in it. In contradiction to, for instance, Karl Barth's gigantic *Church Dogmatics,* it is a minima, i.e., it says only what the author can spell out with integrity and honesty.

In the field of anthropology, Gregor Smith has written a book called *The New Man*,[17] which tries simply to spell out and amplify what Bonhoeffer has said about the Christian being simply a man.

In the field of ethics, Dr. Lehmann[18] wrote a koinonia ethic which deals with the trouble we all have to say what

Christian ethics are. All ethical problems are shared by Christians and non-Christians, the difference being that the Christian comes to them with the understanding and the background of his life and participation in the Christian community. For a clear discussion, this great book should be read in contrast to Herbert Waddams' *A New Introduction to Moral Theology*,[19] which is newer and does not only give a good account of what moral theology wants to say in contrast to a secular ethic like Lehmann's, but also shows (at least to me) that it is exactly the process of secularization and the degree to which it is taken seriously which forms the difference between Lehmann and Waddams.

So much for the theological probings. One could add Roman Catholic names like Küng (*The Structures of the Church*) and Rahner, and even more the names of Schillebeeckx and Hoefnagels.[20]

The other important fruit for the church, which comes directly from this new insight, is the importance of the *structures of the church*.[21] The World Council of Churches has been asking for several years now: What are legitimate and effective structures for a missionary church? Or, to frame the same idea differently: How can the church organize itself in our secular world today so that it does not get in the way between God and man?

The developments in ecclesiology are tremendous. Since we are aware, in many parts of the world, that the old *corpus Christianum* has passed away and that we now have a totally new relationship between church and world in which the body of Christ finally becomes what her Master has always been—a Servant—we discover that the church does not dictate the forms of the society but that the society dictates the forms of the church.

The church, it has now been repeatedly said, is not the goal of the mission of God to his world; it is simply one of the tools which brings together the first fruits of humanity to live out the promised future. These two things—the instrumental function and the representative function of the church—determine the debate. It is impossible to play them out against each other and speak about the mission of the church and the life of the church as two different sides of the same coin. The life and the mission of the church are both instrumental and representative of the reality that God is an active God who goes through history, quietly but definitely.

It should be seen that the quest is for new structures in the plural, which means that there is a new insight that in a pluriform society (which is different from a pluralistic society!) the church can only exist in many forms. The Sunday morning congregation, meaningful for many great traditions and even central in some of them, needs at least to be supplemented with many other ecclesiastical forms of witness, service, and worship, which are no less church and not only extras but which are expressions of the same reality that in the New Testament is also called by many names.[22]

The form that the discussion on structures takes is often the plea for experiments—not only experiments that balance the essentially static nature of the church, but experiments as the normal way in which our scientific and technological society attempts to stay on top of the shaking and accelerating changes that take place.

Experiments in science and technology are the normal way in which progress is made, and they never stop. The end result of one series of experiments is the first factor in a new series of experiments. That is how the church will have to live and, let us not despair, already lives. The old and static forms of church life do not, as we all know, excite people any longer. It is the courageous, experimental thinking and the hopeful, experimental action that keep people alive.

So the process of secularization, ambiguous as it is, can spell freedom to people as well as lay a new yoke upon them. It is up to us, the people of the twentieth century who have chosen to stay with Christ (because to whom should we turn? John 6:68), to use it in freedom and courage.

NOTES

1. Dietrich Bonhoeffer, *Prisoner for God: Letters and Papers from Prison* (The Macmillan Company, 1953), pp. 156 ff.; published in England by SCM Press, Ltd., London, 1953, and Fontana Books, London, 1959, under the title *Letters and Papers from Prison*.

2. Cf. Report of the World Conference for Life and Work, held in Oxford in 1937; and the Encyclical of Pope Pius X, *Lamentabili* (1907).

3. Walter Harrelson, in Martin E. Marty, ed., *The Place of Bonhoeffer* (Association Press, 1962; SCM Press, Ltd., London, 1963).

4. Bonhoeffer, *op. cit.,* pp. 162 f.

5. Cf. D. L. Munby, *The Idea of a Secular Society, and Its Significance for Christians* (Oxford University Press, London, 1963).

6. Harvey Cox, *The Secular City* (The Macmillan Company, 1964; SCM Press, Ltd., London, 1965).

7. A. Th. van Leeuwen, *Christianity in World History* (Edinburgh House Press, London, 1964).

8. Hendrikus Berkhof, *The Doctrine of the Holy Spirit* (John Knox Press, 1964), pp. 101–102.

9. Cf. *Concept,* edited by Hans J. Margull, World Council of Churches. See also Colin W. Williams, *Where in the World?* and *What in the World?* (National Council of Churches, 1963 and 1964).

10. *Student World,* No. 1, 1963.

11. C. F. von Weizsäcker, *Zum Weltbild der Physik,* and *Die Tragweite der Wissenschaft* (Hirzelverlag, Stuttgart, 1956 and 1964 respectively).

12. Martin Jarrett-Kerr, *The Secular Promise* (Fortress Press, 1965; SCM Press, Ltd., London, 1964).

13. John A. T. Robinson, *Honest to God* (The Westminster Press, 1963; SCM Press, Ltd., London, 1963); David L. Edwards, ed., *The Honest to God Debate* (The Westminster

Press, 1963; SCM Press, Ltd., London, 1963). See also Chapter 7, "The *Honest to God* Debate in Ecumenical Perspective" in this book.

14. Paul M. van Buren, *The Secular Meaning of the Gospel* (The Macmillan Company, 1963; SCM Press, Ltd., London, 1963).

15. Ian T. Ramsey, *Religious Language: An Empirical Placing of Theological Phrases* (The Macmillan Company, 1963).

16. Gerhard Ebeling, *The Nature of Faith* (Muhlenberg Press, 1962; William Collins Sons & Co., Ltd., London, 1961).

17. Ronald Gregor Smith, *The New Man: Christianity and Man's Coming of Age* (Harper & Brothers, 1956; SCM Press, Ltd., London, 1955).

18. Paul L. Lehmann, *Ethics in a Christian Context* (Harper & Row, Publishers, Inc., 1963; SCM Press, Ltd., London, 1963).

19. Herbert M. Waddams, *A New Introduction to Moral Theology* (SCM Press, Ltd., London, 1964).

20. Harry Hoefnagels, *Kirche in Veränderter Welt* (Essen, 1964).

21. Williams, *What in the World?* and *Where in the World?;* Gibson Winter, *The Suburban Captivity of the Churches* (Doubleday & Company, Inc., 1961).

22. Paul S. Minear, *Images of the Church in the New Testament* (The Westminster Press, 1960; Lutterworth Press, London, 1961).

II

A WORLD WITHOUT GOD

I AM NOT very fond of pathological remarks, but I could spend half of this chapter speaking about the predicament of our generation (the twenty-five to thirty-five age range) in all continents of the world, and their despair about both their faith and their churches. If you had been in Nairobi, where we had for the first time a youth and student conference for the whole continent of Africa, you would perhaps have shared a remark that Dr. Visser 't Hooft made to us when he came back. "In ten years," he asked, "how many of those young people will still be connected with the Christian church?"—so great was the frustration of those students at the irrelevance of their church and its inability to prepare them for the political and social questions that they face.

Latin America is probably even worse, producing a student generation that sees little or no relation between its faith and its social role, or between the church and its anxieties.

When we speak about "a world without God," that cloud of witnesses is with us, because however disunited and divided this world may be, there is no doubt that any question that is existential is our personal question as well as the question of our whole generation. Therefore, we have vicariously to find the questions and answers for our brethren who live in very different circumstances. We in

Western Europe, whatever we say about ourselves and however sorry we feel for ourselves, are still by far the best off. We are not hungry, not deprived of education, and not thrown into a revolution. That may, of course, mean that we are worse off, because the questioning that goes on in Africa, Latin America, Eastern Europe, and the South of the United States penetrates the existence of the people engaged in it with an intensity that we hardly know.

Allow me to make three preliminary remarks about the topic of this chapter. The first one could come from a large group of people in Eastern Europe. At first hearing, they would call this title blasphemous, giving up the very heart of our belief and denying in Biblical-theological terms both the Shekinah, the indwelling, of God in the Old Testament and the incarnation of God in the New. Many fearful and anti-Communist Christian voices in the West have spoken about Communist countries as a "world without God," a place where the Lordship of Christ is called to a halt by atheistic rule and by absolute materialism. But we have to know that a prophetic minority in the church in the East has reversed the charges and insisted that this evaluation of their situation is the *real* atheism and also the best help to the ideologists of dialectical materialism, because it repeats—or at least seems to repeat—what the official Marxist ideologists have always proclaimed: God is not here. The Communists say he may reign in the West on his throne built on ignorance and preferentialism, but ours is "a world without God"! Our brethren in the East have spoken against that with great clarity. You probably know the little book by Johannes Hamel[1] in which he calls East Germany "God's beloved country," and tries very hard to educate us in the West to see that only *this* faith can produce the endurance by which the ecclesia is revitalized. Whatever we say about "a world without God," we say it in the presence of these brethren who live in the heat of the day, and their struggle will have to have a bearing on our considerations. That is the first qualifying remark on the title.

The second preliminary remark is that "a world without God" has still another connotation. We have to remember that to a lot of people such a title still sounds like a *program* that has yet to be carried out. As we now have slogans such as "A world without hunger" or "A world without war," so there is still the militant school of propagandists of secularism carrying on the program of their founder, George Jacob Holyoake. Holyoake worked out a system of ethical principles on the basis of four presuppositions—emphasis on the material and cultural progress of mankind; respect for the search for truth wherever it may come from; interest for this world and its progress and not for any world to come; an independent, reasonable morality not based on divine imperatives. Holyoake and his followers went on a crusade for freedom from religious control and a courageous search for truth. For us today, their battle sounds very idealistic and very unscientific, even superfluously excitable. But we must remember that, for instance, in Latin America and certainly in the east of Europe, the Holyoakes are still very vocal, and "a world without God" for them is certainly not blasphemy but, on the contrary, is the program to be carried out.

I would say that for us the Holyoakes *have* conquered the Holy Land. The program *is* carried out, and therefore we feel more at home with those who simply approach the world without God phenomenologically, as a statement of fact, as a *self-evident description of reality*.

This, then, is my third qualifying remark on the title. On the Continent, this line of thinking has been clearly expounded by Karl Jaspers, who has a historical interest in secularism as a school of thought, but who has described the process of secularization in the context of the influence of modern European science and technique. He has concentrated very convincingly on our age as a *new* phenomenon, and he used very strong language for that. "The

European science and technique," he says, "are the basically new things, basically and totally different, incomparable with what Asia produced, and even foreign to the Greeks." This is an almost lyrical way of expressing the new age into which we have come. It is a new step in the development of mankind, characterized by its own features.

He mentions the following characteristics: "The universality of science does not accept limits of any kind; its basically unfinished nature with the inherent qualities of flexibility, openness and self-criticism secures progress, but it also threatens the scientist with the consciousness of the, meaninglessness of a process in which all things float and keep changing."

"Science," Jaspers says somewhere else, "is interested in all things. Triviality does not exist for it." Or again: "Science is basically unsystematic, it is unable to create a cosmos of being or a cosmic image which embraces all knowledge. It is unsystematic and it attacks all systems. Scientific questioning is radical. It questions everything down to its roots: even the unimaginable is cooly caught in theoretical mathematics." "And," says Jaspers, "in the modern world a scientific way of thinking has become possible which approaches all reality in the attitude of questioning and research," as he described it above. He knows very well that it is not the *only* way of approaching reality, but that it is the prevailing one for us who live in this day and age. Expressions such as "a given truth" are no longer self-evident philosophical expressions that can be used carelessly; they now indicate a conservative attitude.[2]

I hope and believe that we find the context of our topic here. It is the simple description of our time that draws the face of "a world without God," and before we go on, we have to discover this, to digest it, to be honest about it, and to live with it. The human mind has exegeted God out of the open questions of existence, and in growing up, man has more and more chased the various gods out of their positions of control of human affairs. The process has been a long and slow one. It seems that the time is far away in which gods controlled men through thunderstorms and fire, although in some parts of Europe the fear of nature—not as a giant brute but as an animated and intelligent power—still exists. A little trip through Greece and Latin Europe still shows us the roadside chapels built where a tree was broken by bad weather, or where a house burned down after being struck by "heavenly fire." However, that strikes us as an educational and pastoral concern more than it shows us the divine quality of the weather!

It has also become clear to us that the process of secularization is irreversible. Man will not worship the weather any longer, nor will he again regard politics as the privilege of the king, and the archpriest as the only and plenipotentiary representative of God.

Mankind, in this age or in any age to come, is not going back to the belief that God controls the flu or even cancer, and that in cases of sickness the priest—in his quality of exorcist—has to be consulted rather than the physician.

The people of the Netherlands are not going to pray to God to keep the water from their lowlands, but they will invest more and more public tax money in building higher and better dykes; and that change of action has been developing over the last two hundred years.

Mankind will not go back to the Old Testament for governing principles of how our planet was made, but will go on to trace its physical mysteries with X-rays and microscopes. The time when theology and metaphysics *controlled* our scientific methods is over. Copernicus, Galileo, and Darwin may be corrected and their theories overhauled, but they cannot be ignored or their discoveries undone. And it is that process of ever-growing independence from any transcendent control which has been expressed in words such as "secularization" and "coming of age." We may criticize the terms, we may even dislike what they stand for, but we cannot reverse the process. The world in which we live is forever without a god who has continuous and sovereign control over mankind, without whom we would have no bread, no health, no safety.

We must have heard that argument over and over again, but the interesting thing is that it never really got into our blood. Why do we have to repeat it so often? Why do we have to keep arguing with the theologians who want to defend God from the loss of many of the functions our ancestors ascribed to him? Do we secretly long for the time in which the weight of a woman betrayed her pact with the devil? in which a scientist was burned because he discovered that the earth was not the center of the universe? Do we want the time to come back in which teachers were fired because they corrupted our children with the story that God did not make Adam and Eve out of dust and by blowing in their noses, but that in millions of years life developed from living unicellular entities into the bipeds we are? Do we look back to the time in which a psychologist was excommunicated because he insisted that faith and unbelief were also related to the child's experience with his father and mother and the secretion of his glands? Do we secretly long for a time in which lack of knowledge of the way in which matter moves in its atoms, and the human being could be explained in simple terms of belief and unbelief, was dressed up in the sacred garments of divinity? Or—and to myself this is quite a painful question—is it simply that we are religious people who do not shun a bit of opiate and who have found how useful, for ourselves and for others, a bit of make-believe can be? Are we afraid of our freedom?

Whatever the answer may be to all these beautiful rhetorical questions, could we—before we go on—agree that the title of this chapter is not intended as blasphemy, nor as the foundation of a program of the British Student Christian Movement, but arises out of our experience and is an indication of an irreversible process in which all gods and all metaphysics lost the controlling function that man had previously ascribed to them?

Now let us go on and learn from history that all those people who concentrated their belief in God on those things which man cannot yet master have been refuted. The old attempt of all religions to reserve for the gods certain realms of the world that puzzle us and that still refuse us entrance—such as the weather, or the cause of cancer, or the creation of life—has been proved to be highly dangerous.

In the course of history, theologians have reserved for God all kinds of realms for which he had established the order and which, therefore, man could not change—the distribution of property, civil rights, health and sickness, creation, infallible speaking through Scriptures, and the religious feelings and workings of the soul. But in the course of that same history God lost his hegemony of all these domains.

Man took over distributing property (although in some continents the battle is still going on between the rich defending their possessions in the name of the Divine Distributor and the poor claiming a share of the riches in the name of the equality of all men). But by and large, man took over distributing property.

The French Revolution fired God as the chief political executive of the country who reigned infallibly. Darwin stripped God forever of those creative powers with which he had, until then, made man out of nothing and was believed to have created the earth in six human days, taking a day off on Saturday. Strauss and company sent God home as the oracle who spoke infallibly through Scripture, and they established once and for all that the Bible is a human book that shares confusion and contradiction and an outdated concept of the world with the literature of its time.

Finally, Sigmund Freud *cum suis* attacked the last place of which God was the uncontrollable Lord and Master: the soul, the religious experiences and feelings of the believers.

He fired God as the only one who could penetrate the unconscious and the soul, and made him, at the very best, one of the many occupants of our inner life, where he had to make his dwelling with such earthly companions as libido, trauma, and the subconscious.

These are only examples. The *Honest to God* debate has reminded us that God lost a house "up there" a long time ago, and that his temporary living in a place "out there" has also come to an end. And, with some of its critical participants, I add my doubts that his refuge "in there" is any more safe than any of the previous habitations.

Without wanting to sound snobbish, I must say that the objections against what we call the irreversible process of secularization—in which man takes over the control of most of his own affairs from God—do not much interest me. We all know that there are important things that man does not yet control. We are only at the beginning of our discoveries. But what we know, we know; and the areas that were once reserved for God are so no longer, and they never will be again.

I also know that "man come of age," the real adult, is not a portrait of most people. We all know that lots of people will fall back under new controls because they cannot bear the new freedom. We know that most people would be as secularized as they could be, provided they would only be honest with the facts. I know that 90 percent of mankind stuffs the universe with new gods—but what does it prove? Shall we stack our cards with those who are behind the times?

What does the theologian do with all this? Obviously his first reaction is one of panic and defense. One could write a "Church History of Panic," in which the red thread through the ages is the fight of the Christian apologetics against man's growing independence—a history of stakes, excommunication bulls, the various ways in which all

churches established their indices or withheld their im-
primaturs.

I do not think that we should be too harsh on theology
for being so defensive about traditional beliefs. The church
has no choice but to live in the tension of the other gospel,
the bringer of which is cursed (Gal. 1:9) on the one hand,
and the many more things the Spirit will teach (John
14:26) on the other. It is extremely difficult to discern
where the judgment of the church is orthodox and where
it is conservative, and it is extremely difficult to discern
whether scientific pronouncements are expressions of freedom of the human mind or whether they are already the
buds of a new ideology.

When we look back on the recent past, it is clear that
the theologians were as wrong to battle secularization as
they were right to reject secularism. (Even today it is impossible to go to a conference about secularization without having somebody mix up these two words!) It does
not help much to be freed from religious control and then
to fall head over heels into ideological control. The story
of Communism is a sad example of a freedom gained that
was quickly corrupted into a new dogmatic prison.

We must also say that, by and large, the theologians
have had a flair for recognizing new ideologies and re-
jecting them, at least more than recognizing that their own
systems ideologized the gospel and substituted new laws
of belief for the freedom of the story of revelation.

It must be clear that it has always been a tiny minority
in all ages which, with lucidity and great insight, has discovered the narrow path between freedom and ideology,
between what liberates and what binds, between what is
gospel and what is law. Those men have never been very
popular, because they never swallowed any system or any
discovery wholesale, but very subtly selected the wheat
from the tares and invoked the wrath both of the conservative groups in the churches (who condemned them
for going too far), and of the scientists (who condemned

them for not going far enough). It is that minority of theologians which interests us in this conference, and we have to listen to them very carefully and not waste our time by trying to refute the others.

Let me try to make four points in which theologians have stated the theological position with regard to the process of secularization. (Before I start that, I want the reader to know that I am on a very slippery road, almost using the pastor's trick of nicely analyzing the problem and then claiming it all again for theology and God.)

The first thing we discover is that *it is very difficult to be more revolutionary than the gospel is.* Our title, "A World Without God," is a legitimate expression of the experience of the writers of both the Old Testament and the New.

Remember the words of Job: "Behold, I go forward, and he is not there; and backward, and I do not perceive him. I go to the south to seek him, but I cannot behold him; and turn to the north, and I cannot see him." (Job 23:8–9.)

And remember the parables of our Lord; for instance, Matt., ch. 21, where he said: "Hear another parable. There was a householder who planted a vineyard, . . . let it out to tenants, and *went abroad*" (v. 33).

These are very difficult texts, but in some way or other both are unmistakably covered by our title. I know that these two quotations do not depict *our* questions, but at least they mean that our problems are not so new as many of us always think! The idea that this world is without a God who controls all behavior and all life is not un-biblical at all. The Bible, as we all know, is a complicated book that resists systematization into one clear doctrinal expression of what it describes. But it must be said that the hidden, the silent, the forsaking, or the absent are as much categories in which the witnesses of the revelation have described the life with JHWH as the present, the revealed, the speaking, and the coming. It is hard to be more secular (earthbound) than the Old Testament, and even more difficult to interpret the New Testament as a Baedeker for the road to heaven.

The second remark is that *the story of the self-disclosure of JHWH, the revelation of JHWH, is not only secular but also secularizing.* It has been pointed out repeatedly that revelation of God is a secular action; it means that even in the prescientific language of the Bible the holy merges with the profane and so produces the secular. The *shalom* of God—the peace, or the salvation, or however you want to translate that very central word in the Old and New Testaments—the *shalom* of God (which includes all earthly things such as justice, and good, and peace, and freedom, and righteousness) is given and measured in social and political categories and has only transcendent qualities in this way. Whatever you say about what happens in the Bible between Israel and JHWH, and between Jesus and Israel, the pagans and the nations, it is clear that the Bible uses very secular language. It does that to such an extent that Biblical literature—literarily speaking—has much less standing than many other religious writings, and catches the divine "in-coming" into this world in political, social, secular terms.

But that is not all. It is also secularizing. The apologetic sermon of creation in Genesis, which was written much more as a refutation of creation stories with which Israel was confronted in exile than as an independent effort to produce a scientific explanation of the universe, at least establishes the independence of man. Adam is a person *coram Deo,* before God; he is another person. He is an entity in himself, and therefore potentially free. The sermon of Gen., ch. 3, explaining the mystery of sin, proclaims at the same time man's freedom to transgress — he *can* do that — and his "being thrown into the world" which he will have to make useful. All meditations in early Genesis established both man's freedom and God's freedom.

I do not think that we distort the Old Testament when we read it as the tale of a fight between the religiosity of man and the otherness of JHWH. Both are there. It is not direct God-written revelation; it was edited and changed many times and bears the marks of human attempts to make JHWH bearable to live with. But it also bears the unmistakable mark of an insight that will not have JHWH domesticated, smoothed over, or accommodated to our human desire.

Modern scholarship has taught us that there has been a growth in Israel's understanding of JHWH and his Kingship. That growth is not that Israel more and more experienced its God as the fulfillment of their best longings, or as the only sure thing they possessed, the ground of their being, or as the way they could best be certain about their earthly life. On the contrary, the growth in Israel's understanding of JHWH was a discovery that he was different, over against them and especially over against their religion. The Temple, as Israel's climactic expression of religion, is attacked time and time again in the prophetic tradition of Israel's life. The Old Testament, especially in the prophetic facets, is highly secular and highly secularizing. The cult of Israel and its professionals and its buildings are severely attacked in favor of a relation to JHWH that expresses itself in righteousness and social commitment. The image of God that corresponds to this is one of majesty, revealed in weakness and lowliness. The progress in Israel's understanding of JHWH is a progress in understanding that his majesty is revealed in terms of weakness and lowliness. The tension between these two is the heart of Israel's life with JHWH.

The New Testament simply intensifies this development and focuses it on the Rabbi Joshua of Nazareth. Here also JHWH is recognized as revealing himself as a servant, whose function is to serve rather than to be the venerable center of religion to be served. Certainly in the New Testament, God is hidden, God is abroad, God is waiting; and the core of the message is that he reveals himself in a man who refuses to show his divinity. And therefore, all religion,[3] which certain Jewish schools of theology had carefully built up, breaks on this man. Through this man it became unmistakably clear that it is impossible to speak of God as one of the gods, but that here one is unique, of another kind.

The religion of the Jews broke on this man because the fixed system was attacked. Let me make that clear in four points. The *fixed place* (the Temple) is used by Rabbi Joshua, but never made compulsory. On the contrary, his followers will worship neither here nor in Jerusalem, and the Temple has to crumble. The *fixed time* of religion— the Sabbath—is profaned in the sense of the official theology of the day and used for recreation, both in the sense of leisure time and of healing. The *fixed group* to which one had to belong to acquire salvation (Israel) is opened up; salvation is no longer tied up with belonging to the right people. Many will come from East and West, and his followers will go into the unclean houses of the *Gojjim* unto the ends of the earth. The *fixed morality,* in which tax collectors are excommunicated and adulterers are executed, gives way to *an ethical behavior in which love and mercy are the chief elements in a strict but experimental discipline.* "Strict discipline" is important in that phrase.

The heart of the teaching of the Rabbi Joshua is to be found in his parables, which are also the simple vignettes of life which Christians have proclaimed them to be. But apart from that, they are very precise pronouncements of Israel's history, the central event of God's revelation and the predicament of man. The world of the parables is "a world without God" in which the test given to man is precisely that of living *etsi Deus non daretur*—as if God did not exist. We should understand that phrase rightly. It does not say we should live as we do *quia Deus non daretur*—because God does not exist—but it says that just because he is this God who goes abroad and leaves the vineyard to his servants, he requires this life of faith which is lived as seeing the invisible by those who have not seen and still believe. That means living like the Messiah, who renounced all claims on heavenly troops.

The history of revelation is not the story of the growing visibility of God, but on the contrary, the history of revelation is the story of the opposite. The action of God, as portrayed in the Bible, is one in which the audio-visual aids are progressively reduced so that man may learn to live in faith as the only and lasting reality. Circumcision, the Mosaic law, the Temple, the physical presence of the God-man Jesus—they all go; and what is left is the open, flexible, and daily-renewed community of those who are preserving in the Spirit the story and the faith, in the face of all evidence to the contrary.

When we speak about the Lordship of Christ, and try to listen to that in this secular and secularizing understanding of JHWH and his Rabbi Joshua, we must therefore say firstly that the process of secularization has not stopped. I am willing to venture the thesis that the Lordship of Christ is seen and experienced exactly in secularization. We should remember that the story of the gospel being carried into the different continents of the world is a story of the secularization of each of those continents. Wherever the Christian faith is proclaimed and *lived out,* gods tumble. The moment the mission built a hospital in Central Africa, gods were fired. We have to live for a long time with that past period, but when the gospel was carried to Asia, in its funny form of the scientific freedom that man had gained through the ages in Europe and North America, the religions may resurge as much as they want, but they will undergo the secularizing influence of the gospel; and if we read between the lines of the story of Rabbi Joshua of Nazareth, we cannot expect anything else. To say it in traditional language—when Jesus mounted his throne and all power was given to him (Phil. 2:9–10), it became clear that the gods had no place left—not even the gods Christianity had made up for itself to preserve the church, or a Christian continent, or anything else contrary to the gospel.

In all that, we should remember that the despair of Thomas, who had to touch before he could believe, is mild in comparison to our own situation. Thomas did not doubt the existence of JHWH, the details of creation did not bother him, the ambivalence of all religious language was unknown to him, the essential independence of man was still clouded by lack of knowledge, the earth stood safely in the center of the universe, and psychological processes in his own soul did not bother him a bit. But since then all those things have gone, and we are stripped of more certainties than he was, and one of them is that we have been stripped of the certainty of religion. There is no discussion as to whether this is bad or good. The Bible is a book in which religion is *allowed,* but it does not become the intermediary between God and man.

My third remark is that *theology*—if it is true theology and not "religiology"—*rejoices in this process*. It could not expect anything else to happen. It will not defend the position of old with dubious argument, but recognizes that fire was indeed thrown on the earth and many things were burned. And we know that in Jesus' time the religious people—the systematizers—could not take it. This is hard language, they said. Who can listen to it? Nor could the Jewish-Christian congregation in Jerusalem take it, and it tried to substantiate faith with food laws and circumcision.

Paul encountered the same attempts in Colossae, where the Christians could not take it in their gnostic syncretistic environment and insisted on some fixed pattern of worship or observation of the law. Let us listen to Paul refuting this, and let us hear him say to the Colossians and to all those who could not take that hard language against religion: "You were buried with him in baptism, in which you were also raised with him through faith in the working of God. . . . Therefore let no one pass judgment on you in questions of food and drink or with regard to a festival or a new moon or a sabbath. These are only a shadow of what is to come; but the substance belongs to Christ. Let no one disqualify you, insisting on self-abasement and worship of angels, taking his stand on visions, puffed up without reason by his sensuous mind, and not holding fast to the Head, from whom the whole body, nourished and knit together through its joints and ligaments, grows with a growth that is from God. If with Christ you died to the elemental spirits of the universe [religion included], why do you live as if you still belonged to the world? Why do you submit to regulations, 'Do not handle, Do not taste, Do not touch' . . . , according to human precepts and doctrines? These have indeed an appearance of wisdom in promoting rigor of devotion and self-abasement and severity to the body, but they are of no value in checking the indulgence of the flesh." (Col. 2:12, 16–23.)

Ever since then, however, men have attempted to conceal the nakedness of faith (although, of course, theologians have always talked about it) with laws, systems, cathedrals, and ministries; and it seems that only in our century is it all put to the test. What God could not do through the right hand of his church, he had to do through the left hand of science, atheism, the analysis of language, and the people's loss of the organ of religion. We realize now that God went abroad and left the vineyard to us— and it is to us in the plural. It is good to remind ourselves that we have nothing left but each other, and that therefore the thing we have to work out from there is *the mystery of communal life.*

Fourthly, I realize very well that I have been on that slippery path of trying to reclaim all we have lost before we have really lived through the abandonment. Therefore, let me underline even more strongly that we still have to do the painful job of rethinking our whole faith in secular terms and redefining all our attitudes to our heritage and to the task of today and tomorrow. We should also insist that the question be put in its proper theological context.

Let me close with a qualifying remark on the job that is ahead. *"A world without God"* is certainly not a world *without the ecclesia.* The servants are called to take care of the vineyard. We may as well know and remember immediately that—according to the Rabbi Joshua, whose students we are—many do not and many will not do this. The call to the servants is not to find God's address abroad: the call is to look after the vineyard. And the vineyard is the world. For me, Bonhoeffer remains the man who has most penetratingly written up the predicament of the vineyard and the task of the servant in it. We should then remember (and that is painful) that Bonhoeffer was not one of the perplexed Christians of today who have no discipline left and who feel lost in both the modern world and the traditional church. Of course, all the people without discipline claim him, but he himself was an aristocrat of discipline, who—precisely because of this—was able to live a religionless Christianity and call for it in others. Religionless Christianity stands for a life in which *security* is given up, but in which *certitude* is trained in a life of prayer and fellowship.

That is, in a way, a very simple program, so simple that it is very hard to hear. On the basis of the existence of men (though not all men), those men who do not have a hook left to hang their religion on, who are not moved by hymns, garments, services, and systems, and who indeed despair of traditional church life and traditional theologizing, he pleads for a total renewal of both. In that, he is not alone. There is in this world a whole company of people who have seen that the plea for today is a plea for total renewal.

I think that it is time to concentrate on that second pregnant word in Bonhoeffer's thought, after we have done a lot of homework on the religionless Christianity, although we may not all understand it in the same terms. It is now time to see what he means by the *Arkanadisziplin,* the hidden discipline, and for that we will have to do some of the things we have been hearing for years that we should do. We have to form cells; we have to start from scratch; we should get young and old, clerical and lay, trained secularly and theologically; all those people who shout *Hallelujah!* whenever a book or an article appears in which total renewal is demanded or specific measures or schemes of renewal are advocated—we should get them together. We should get them together in small groups, and *work*. We have all read our *Soundings*,[4] our *Objections to Christian Belief*,[5] our *Honest to God*,[6] proving that we have lots of good people working entirely on their own. The need is for calling them together and making them study and speak together. Bonhoeffer taught us that in "a world without God" the few Christians left should find each other for a common life of prayer, study, and observing the signs of the times.

The Son of Man, when he comes back, shall he find faith? (Luke 18:8.)

NOTES

1. Johannes Hamel, *A Christian in the DDR* (Association Press, 1960; SCM Press, Ltd., London, 1960).

2. Karl Jaspers, *Vom Ursprung und Ziel der Geschichte*, Part II (Fischer, Frankfurt-Hamburg, 1955).

3. One cannot use the word "religion" anymore without giving one's own explanation of it. I, following Bonhoeffer, hold religion to be man's response to God turned into a system, or faith turned ideology, the refusal to serve and insist that God should be served. It is the individualistic concern for salvation or the dependence on a *deus ex machina*.

4. Alexander R. Vidler, ed., *Soundings: Essays Concerning Christian Understanding* (Cambridge University Press, 1962).

5. D. M. MacKinnon, *et al.*, *Objections to Christian Belief* (J. B. Lippincott Company, 1964; Constable & Co., Ltd., London, 1963).

6. Robinson, *Honest to God*.

III

THE HUMILIATION OF THE CHURCH

I HAD QUITE a time preparing this essay. What I wanted to do first of all was to quote one of the recognized leaders of the renewal of the church: a quotation that would at the same time unmask the church as largely irrelevant in the world of today and show that the only way left is total renewal—a renewal not only of the wallpaper but of the walls of the church (a remark I borrow from Ernest Southcott).

So I took from my bookshelves the little book by Eberhard Muller that came out right after the war, *The World Has Become Different*,[1] and simply thumbed from there through what I call the "renewal theologians"—Wickham and Wentland, the men who have been speaking about the church in an industrial society; the theologians of renewal, Visser 't Hooft, Rahner, Küng; the laity men, Kraemer, Weber, Congar; the political men, MacLeod and Gollwitzer; the sociologists, Gibson Winter, Peter Berger, Hans Storck; the apostolate and mission people, Hoekendijk, Newbigin, Margull; the people who speak about the relation of religion and society, Abrecht, de Vries. And after that I went through the reports of the great ecumenical meetings, where one finds lots of that stuff. I got so intrigued I forgot to find my quote!

We know that all these people in the end, oddly enough, say the same thing; and it is a fascinating process to thumb quickly through books and not get bogged down by reading. The rediscovery of the Bible, rediscovery of the laity, rediscovery of the church's ministry in politics, rediscovery of the church's mission, rediscovery of the church's community life, and so on. When one goes through one's "renewal" library quickly, it seems as if all these books are made up out of the same basic recipe—take a cup of changed world, a teaspoonful of despair about the actual situation of the church, and half a pound of request for total renewal.

First, the changed world. The fundamentally changed world, as Jaspers has called it,[2] the irrelevance of the church, and the challenge of renewal—that is what today binds together a group of men who are not bound by any other thing. It is not age which binds them. You will find men who are waiting for death, and men who—humanly speaking—have a life before them. They are certainly not bound by confession—Lutherans, Presbyterians, Anglicans, and Romans for once sing the same tune. They are not even bound by culture—Germans and Anglo-Saxons find each other here, which is quite a miracle. They form a group that cuts across all known barriers and other groups. David Edwards has called them the radicals.[3] I would rather call them the *renewal* theologians, because of the prominence of that word in their thinking.

It is very difficult to say precisely where they were born. It may be safest to say that their manger stood at the crossroad of Biblical theology and sociology. It is almost like Luke, ch. 2: in the ordinary houses there was no place for them. Only where people were willing to take a look at the new world in which we find ourselves—the technological, industrial metropolis, where urbanization and neuroses are wed—only there could this kind of theology emerge. And only where all things that had been believed for ages were once again tested against the primal document of our faith, and where—often with a lump in their throats or reluctantly—theologians accepted modern scholarship and bravely rethought what was handed over to them, could the call to total renewal come about.

So they discovered that the humiliation of the church is twofold. She is humiliated because the way in which she is described and sketched in the New Testament is denied by what she actually shows. The attractiveness, the love the people had for her, the unity, the uniqueness over against all human forms of community, is lost. Or worse, when the New Testament lashes out at the "unchurch"—the complacent community of Laodicea, for instance, in The Revelation of John, or the unloving goats of Matt., ch. 25, or the man who did not forgive although he was himself forgiven (Matt., ch. 18)—it seems that a sharp and merciless photograph of our churches is presented to us.

The second humiliation—which in a way is only the other side of the coin—is her *increasing* irrelevance in the world of which she is a part: her irrelevance and conservatism in the world of politics, economy, and even charity; her irrelevance in the racial and colonial and welfare struggle of most of mankind; her irrelevance for the youth of developing countries; her Babylonian captivity in the armament race; her feeble speaking in the moral struggle of today; her spiritual poverty in an age of haste and neuroses. *The church, paralyzed and mute because of her divided state, is humiliated because she is neither what she professes to be nor what she is told to be.*

This is what the renewal theologians discovered together. This is what they have taught since the war—and they have been heard. We should not be so cynical as to say that they have been crying in the wilderness—not at all. In the years between 1945 and 1955, all over Europe at least, experiments were springing up. Germany was punctuated by lay academies; Bible study groups sprang up in each country; house churches were experimented with; industrial experiments were taken on; youth work experiments were the order of the day; liturgical renewal made itself heard; and ecumenical councils, the World Council of Churches, and ecumenical committees started to work hard on battling against the disunity of the church.

What happened to this great company of renewers was that the church applauded them—they had a great audience; their books sold. It went even farther: although *all* those men pleaded for a revolution, a total renewal, new walls, church leaders were so careless as to recommend them to their theological students—and we read them. People borrowed their books and did not give them back. For a long time it has been very difficult, for instance, in the Netherlands, to get a secondhand copy of the Wickham book,[4] a thing quite unheard of in theological literature. They became, and still fill, the "abundance" corner of our libraries, as against the "bankruptcy" corner of the "Aid to Prayer" books MacLeod speaks about in that classic book *Only One Way Left.*[5] They were books and men that gave us hope and strength.

But then the great disappointment came. Praise for renewal theology appeared to be largely lip service. It is a scandal to see the beautiful ecumenical documents which the churches drew up together far away from the place where God had set them and which were never applied at home. If somebody has sufficient courage to make a study of cynicism, he should buy the reports of all major ecumenical gatherings, read them, and see what the churches said together. Then he should go to the balcony of his house and look over his city at the churches that are standing there, from which steeples have risen to heaven since the Middle Ages, and see how nothing has happened to them.

Lay training centers in Europe were largely domesticated. Built as places where Christians were trained for their lonely experiments of faith in the world, they became instruction houses for the churches' middle class. The house church experiments in many places stopped. Youth work experiments in many places stopped, or—after a courageous beginning—they often turned into proselytizing fishing ponds and were then stopped when no converts were made. The Bible study circles, which were so numerous in the first years after the war, dwindled because Bible study is difficult. No church in the whole world really practically applied the new partnership of the laity and the clergy, advocated in all corners of our sanctuaries. Instead of *doing* it, we made it a conference topic and the title for the bishop's best lecture. When we look back at the period since 1945, we see the renewal movement imprisoned in carefully defined and tentative experiments which were never allowed to become a strategy. We see courageous new initiatives domesticated, and others stopped because they were dangerous; some were institutionalized, and only a handful are still swimming against the stream of easy restoration.

When the world changed around us, the churches remained the same. There is not one industrial hymn in our hymnbooks. We sing gaily about birds and horses and other rural niceties, but cars, tractors, airplanes, and machines are left to the newspapers. The structures, the walls of the churches, stand as always. Certainly denominations have become ecumenical denominations, but they still remain denominations. Laymen are now partners, but remain sheep. Lay academies are called laboratories for worldly holiness, but become schools for churchgoers. And the liturgical renewal—instead of fulfilling the promise of an adequate form of worship for modern industrial man— exchanged the word "thine" for "yours" and produced the restoration of the best they had, with a tiny handful of new hymns and tunes that can be used only in conferences because in the forever-standing church buildings of yesterday they indeed sound out of place.

The result is an ever-increasing and ever-continuing exodus of our best laymen and pastors, the growing sense of conservatism among many who despair of total renewal, and so we feel that we may as well make the best of what we have. There is a terrific frustration among those who stayed and who still feel God in the structure of the church. That is not something I made up, but I quote the words of our churches together in ecumenical assemblies—the out-dated structure of the church has apparently been stronger than the renewal of theology.

My topic is the humiliation of the church, and let me start again as if I had not spoken.

All theology for Christians (I say Christians, because Islam also has a theology, of course) starts from Christo-logical considerations. That means that everybody in the Christian church who starts to think about the faith of the Christian community has no other point of departure than the life and teachings of Jesus of Nazareth as handed over to us by church and Scripture. Ecclesiology (the doctrine of the church, thinking about the church) can therefore never be an independent discipline but will always be a part of Christology. In normal language, if we want to think about the church, we have to start thinking about Jesus again.

If, therefore, we look for the constitution of the Chris-tian church, its Magna Carta, we shall find it where the New Testament sings the famous hymn about Jesus (Phil. 2:5–11): "That this disposition be with you which was also in Jesus Messiah who made himself nothing, assuming the nature of a slave, bearing the human likeness, and humbled himself." To sum up in the three focus words of that text: emptiness, service, and solidarity.

Therefore, if that is the constitution of the Christian church, there can be no coexistence of church and world in which they are both independent entities with their own rules, their own powers, and an exchange of ambassadors. But there should be *pro*-existence—that word which was coined and has become so popular on the other side of the Iron Curtain. Pro-existence—the church which is there for the world, on behalf of the world, for the welfare of the world. *I cannot accept any other starting point for thinking about the church.* That is where we have to start —these three words. All the rest we have to say is an attempt to apply this. We are not going to be political realists, seeing what can be done; we are not going to start from what we would like to do or feel like doing. We start from these three basic words of the Messianic alibi, describing our Lord and therefore his church.

The church proves her identity by existing for others, and it is only there that she gets her authority. If she thinks of keeping her own life, she has lost it already. We are not more than our Master, and we therefore take on the *morphē tou doulou,* the form of service. The church is a slave girl in Biblical language, like her Master, existing for others: not only preparing to be there for others, but *being* there for others; she cannot exist for her own benefit. She has to be among men for men. She cannot get out of the world to prepare herself for service. Of course, much of our introverted self-serving is excused with the statements that we do all this only to prepare ourselves to serve the world. All our women's groups, our youth work, our choir practices, our liturgy, our social nights—they all serve our service, which will start when we have become strong. Or so we say. But the New Testament description of the church is different. Slave girls are trained on the job!

The humiliation of the church is her *raison d'être,* and the humiliation of the church that we spoke of in the first half of my remarks—the real humiliation—is that we refuse to be humiliated. Imagine what would happen if the church really listened to the New Testament description and lived up to her existence of being bought and put to work as a slave girl of mankind. That is the challenge we have to live up to. Only in this way will we discover what is called the glorious life of the children of God. Only in this perspective do the questions of renewal and ecumenicity, and the lay question, and all those other domestic questions we have in the church and should clear up become legitimate.

I could think of the most horrifying ecumenical church, in which all laymen were partners of the ministers, and in which all ministers were servants to the laity, and in which we would all be one, and in which we would have the most glorious liturgy that human ears have ever heard, and in which all the problems of the church would be solved, and people would marvel at its greatness and its I-don't-know-what. And it could be totally illegitimate—that church could be a dominant, self-imposing institute and not the slave girl of the New Testament. "Therefore you, like the Master, have this in mind, that he became like men, stooped down to the service of a slave, and therefore was . . . ," and so on.

The tragedy of most renewal experiments of the years after the war was that they tried to educate stronger people rather than people who serve. Many of the renewal experiments were done to make Christian people stronger than the others, to arm them for the evil day, to help them escape suffering with the world, to give them a better life than that of the others. They did not educate for service, but helped people escape the problems of our society.

The tragedy of most Christian youth work was that we tried to shield young people from the world around them, and that we tried to make them into something like "super-youth," who were different, who were distinguished, who were better, who were greater, who did not have all the frustrations, who could master life, and so on. We chose that rather than a Christian youth work that is education for service, and rather than telling them that the place where they belong, where they can meet the Lord, where they can make their baptism function, is there where he is to be found in the likeness of men.

Here let me make a parenthetical remark. Jesus never became a Christian; he became a man. Therefore we are not called to become Christians, and we are not called to create Christians. Our calling is to help people to

become men, and a real man—in the words of Bonhoeffer
—is not somebody who takes his manhood lightly but
who lives with the notions of death and resurrection.

The gospel is the story of the Rabbi Joshua, who
shared people's life. He did not just share the flesh—
which in itself would already be quite something—but
he shared the homelessness of the conscripted at his
birth, the excommunication of the tax gatherer, the loneliness of the excommunicated sinners, the temptation of
all to make things visible and to call for miracles. He
shared the death of the criminal, and it is in this process
of sharing that he frees men from their loneliness, from
their guilt, and carries their temptation and their death.

The story of the gospel is the story of the humility of
God, who renounces his majesty and his almightiness and
all his supernatural qualities. The style of living of the
Messianic community can therefore be no other, but must
be—in Bonhoeffer's words—the story of those who par-
ticipated in the powerlessness of God. Our task is clear.
Jesus asked: Couldn't you stay awake with me one hour?
(Matt. 26:40.)

The church is called to participate in God's suffering
in a Godless world, says Bonhoeffer. The task of the
church can therefore be described in the words "to be
awake with Jesus," to participate in the powerlessness of
God in the world—standing where his power is least evi-
dent, present among the suffering, carrying their sorrow,
choosing for the outlawed. Only he, says Bonhoeffer, only
he who shouts for the Jews is allowed to use the
Gregorian chants! The theme of being awake with Jesus
plays an important role in Bonhoeffer's thought. It means
a resolute "No" to all the tranquilizers our denominations
offer us to sleep in the *status quo* of our irrelevant church
life.

There is no easy answer. There is no cheap grace. The
full price of discipleship has to be paid. The slave nature
of the church must mean that we let the world impose

on us the structures in which we can serve rather than that we impose our structures upon the world—and the latter is in fact what we have done. We impose our structures on all people—even on the pagans, if we still can. Instead of taking the *morphē tou doulou,* the form of the slave, we have mostly taken *one* structure—which was once relevant and which once served—and have made it ultimate and final.

If we look at our churches, we suffer from morphological fundamentalism—fundamentalism of the form that in the end is a refusal to live historically. We base ourselves on the past instead of being serious about living toward the future. Gabriel Marcel said that beautifully: "The Church remembers her future." Taking the form of a slave means letting the world have its own forms and filling those forms with the content of the gospel. Therefore, sociology is essential for the church—it is not helpful, it is essential. Without it we cannot renew our structures. It describes the house in which the slave works.

Hans Storck[6] has very sharply pointed out that the church can be really present and function in a culture only if she synchronizes her *calendar* with the calendar of that society. This is a clear argument, because if we keep our calendar and the world keeps its own, we become a strange body in it, and that is exactly the thing we have always tried to avoid. In the religious, stable society of yesterday, the church imposed its calendar on the people —festivals had to be observed, the Sabbath had to be celebrated, and church bells told people when to pray their morning and evening prayers at the same hours as the monks got up and went to bed.

Of course urbanization and mobility, shift work, and all the changes of our world have done away with a lot of these things because they simply do not work anymore. First of all, the morning and evening prayers. We have left them to the monks. When the calendar of the world changed from a six-day working week to a five-day working week, the world lost Sunday as the indication of the rhythm in which it lives. We have a weekend, and people use it very differently. For a large portion of the population it means the time in which the mobility of society can be celebrated. More and more people will find recreation possibilities that take them away for the whole weekend. The religious celebration of Sunday, already heavily attacked by previous secular possibilities, will once again be the victim. The question is: What will the churches do? Will they keep imposing their Sunday and its observances on the new society, or will they study seriously what a new society asks of them and act accordingly? Would the Christian church really suffer from, for instance, ten "Christ days" in a year and a few weekends, which could take the place of the Sunday observance as we now see it disappear more and more around us?

The question of the Christian calendar has many facets. Let me just mention religious instruction as another example. Most churches inherited the religious instruction system they now have from the stable society where, during one hour a week, the younger age group came together for teaching—and that was a service to them, it was functional. In a modern, largely unstable society, the students come without a sense of community and without the inner coherence of the stable forms of yesterday, and therefore the teaching possibilities are very different. A friend of mine found that three weekends spent with his young people gave more time for coherent instruction *in a context* than the old system with its haphazard and interrupted hours. His church session, however, said that by going away on weekends he neglected both the teaching and the preaching ministry of his church.

This last imposition brings me to a more basic one, namely, the one of *authority*. The authority of the hierarchy in the stable society is unquestioned. The priest (or the minister, or the bishop) is the best-educated man around; he is learned; he is the politician; he is the only administrator of his region (his diocese or his parish). That age, however, as we have all experienced, is now over (even if a few survivors of the old days try to keep us from believing it). Not only has the minister or the priest lost his lonely place of authority to much better educated persons, but the nature of authority itself in our society has become different. In a scientific century such as ours, not all people will be scientific but most of them will live in accordance with the prevailing spirit of the time; and that spirit of science *questions everything* and does not accept any authority that is not recognized or made felt as such. A church that goes on *dictating truths* rather than sitting with the people and working out the real questions is certainly not living in solidarity with the men of today. (I am not suggesting that there are no truths, or that the church does not know them. I only suggest that modern people do not understand *given truths*. We in our time—whether we like it or not, whether we are reluctant or not—have to start from scratch.)

Therefore, religious instruction cannot be given with a simple catechism book any longer. The question-and-answer period has to be replaced by the question-after-question period, in which the answer may be found, the question may disappear, or the questions may stand unanswered. Until now, the authority concept of most of our churches has been imposed; we talk because we know. And we hardly know how painful this is to those who listen to us. In our actions they do not recognize many consequences of our "knowledge," and the answers we give frequently answer questions that we were not asked in the first place.

Next, do we not often impose our group system on the people? The whole debate on the parochial system, or, rather, the parish as *the* structure of the church *par excellence,* shows that we are reluctant to modify an inherited and, at least, deficient structure. Industrial congregations, student congregations, congregations according to profession, class, age, or responsibility, remain experiments. We have inherited from the stable society the notion that people live where they sleep. The mobile society—with its multiform communities in which living, working, recreation, and studying are all done in different places, and in which almost everybody belongs to many (secular) congregations at once—has not yet reached the church. By what we do, and especially by what we plan (think of our church buildings!), we show our intention of concentrating on people's nights rather than their days. The church as a slave girl has become a baby-sitter for the evenings. When will the day come on which the church will rediscover its calling and indeed be free to reorganize its structure in accordance with what society is asking?

The imposition of the service concept can also be worked out with regard to the denominations. How long will we force our denominational structures on the younger churches far away and the young churchmen nearby? Of course it is stupid to make a plea to ignore the denominational differences, but when 30,000 people go into a new housing estate, when teams start working in developing countries, when cities grow and grow, do we not all agree that we all need new forms, and that neither our buildings, our ministries, our liturgies, nor our orders are sufficient? Where shall we start if not in these new ventures? But up until today we have repeated in stone our dividing denominations, and with an ecumenical hymn on our lips, we dedicate faithful copies of yesterday's churches and suffer from their emptiness afterward.

We impose rather than serve. We impose things and customs that were once functional and really served the people, and so we made them the only permissible form, the only genuine trademark of the article we are selling. Whoever attacks this morphological fundamentalism is accused of abusing the tradition, of breaking down the ecclesia itself. So many of the renewers, who were merely pleading for a continuous restructuring of the church so that it could really be a serving church, gave up.

Each new generation is faced with a choice. Will it call for renewal, or will it be satisfied with yesterday—with hymns sung in yesterday's churches on the day that was yesterday's Sabbath? For the renewers, the only way left is the application of Bonhoeffer's phrase, "We shall never know what we do not do." They can only go out for experiment with all they have. Let those who are satisfied with the old structure live in it, but let them not hinder the others from working out their calling in today's world. Let those who worship happily on Sundays do so happily, but let them not hinder the others who live their koinonia in less traditional forms and on less traditional days. Let those who can still stand the heat of the day with their traditional confessions of faith do so, but let them rejoice in those who are for the total rethinking of all they know. Those who know should not laugh at those who do not know much any longer. The unity of the church has to be kept between the traditionalists (in the best sense of that word) and the renewers. Both can claim legitimacy in the community of Jesus, but both should recognize that they exist only by the grace of the other!

NOTES

1. Eberhard Muller, *Die Welt ist anders geworden* (Hamburg, 1953).
2. Jaspers, *Vom Ursprung und Ziel der Geschichte*, Part II, p. 82.
3. See the preface to *The Honest to God Debate*.
4. Edward R. Wickham, *Church and People in an Industrial City* (Lutterworth Press, London, 1957).
5. George MacLeod, *Only One Way Left* (The Iona Community, Glasgow).
6. Hans Storck, *Die Zeit drängt* (Käthe Vogt Verlag, Berlin, 1957).

IV

EXPERIMENTAL PREACHING

"This is Scotland: and there is no lack of hills and rocks, of little streams and waterfalls; and two hundred yards off, winding around that churchyard whose white stones you see by glimpses through old oak branches, a larger river glides swiftly by.

"It is a quiet and beautiful scene, and it pleases me that Britain has thousands and thousands like it. But of course none, in my mind, equal this: for this has been my home for five years."[1]

So begins a book that was anonymously published just ninety years ago under the title *The Recreations of a Country Parson*. The author muses on: "I have been sitting here for an hour, with a book on my knee; and upon that a piece of paper, wheron I have been noting down some thoughts for the sermon which I hope to write during this week, and to preach next Sunday in that little parish church of which you can see the corner of a gable through the oaks which surround the church-yard. . . . Several times, I have been obliged to get up and make a dash at a very small weed which I discerned just appearing through the gravel; and once or twice my man-servant has come to consult me about matters connected with the garden and the stable. My sermon will be the better for these interruptions."[2]

Ninety years is not a very long time. There are,

probably, still people alive who were baptized by the author of these marvelous lines, and maybe the children of his manservant, caught by the bucolic and gracious ministry of the author, have become preachers themselves. Ninety years is a short span, a lifetime of one generation, just long enough to test the real value of a work of art or for a bottle of good wine to mature into a superb one.

And yet, how totally outdated is our Scottish country parson with all his contemporaries all over the world. Since he jotted down his thoughts on a piece of paper, his world seems to have exploded. His manservant disappeared; his children have had no chance to grow up following his example.

The books on the knees of country parsons have changed tone since 1876! In 1883 it was Nietzsche's *Thus Spake Zarathustra.* New Testament scholars like Strauss and Bauer, Schweitzer and Bultmann, produced more and more material that made our Scotsman look rather out of place and out of date. And today we preachers sit in our studies surrounded by books that hardly inspire us to the friendly, careless attitude displayed in the garden.

The exegetical works call for a concentration of study that the telephone hardly allows. The sociological handbooks, which we all buy out of a sort of pastoral masochism, depict on page after page how marginal our whole situation has become and how impossible it is, with one address, to reach a congregation in which so many different social roles and so many conflicting types of experience are represented. The psychological material, highly recommended in seminary, does not exactly encourage the preacher. How much harm is an authoritative word (or a word without authority) going to do to that turmoil of spiritual uncertainties which each person represents?

And then there are our modern artists, writers, and poets. What does a man preach to a group that recognize themselves in the characters described by Baldwin, Murdoch, Snow, Mauriac, and Böhl? What kind of sermon does one preach if the cast of one of Osborne's plays or Fellini's films were to be in the church? And although few of *them* are likely to turn up, we know that our pews are full of people who could easily be typecast in these parts. Or, even more difficult, what if the people in our congregation do not recognize the expressions of our modern culture, but indignantly reject them as unclean and pornographic? What, then, do we say on Sunday morning?

So there he sits, the modern preacher, and meditates. He thinks of all the places where the Word was (and is) preached objectively and to great congregations, and where its impact was painfully little. What did all that undoubtedly orthodox preaching in Germany do to stop the Nazi terror? How was it possible that people could listen devoutly to the kerygma, while in the same street the ruins of the synagogue were still smoldering and the whip lashed out in the concentration camps? How could the solid Calvinistic Dutchman be uplifted by good Reformed preaching, while the Jews were hustled out of his country to a well-known destination? How, in the South of the United States and in South Africa (both regions of well-known Christian religiosity), could the millions of sermons fail to show the world the impact of God becoming a lowly man?

Sittler has pointed out the other obstacles to our preaching: the ever-expanding managerial duties of the parish minister. He speaks of the maceration of the minister. "His studies," he says, "become less and less an occupation engaged in or intrinsic to his role as witness to the gospel and pastor to people, and become more and more frantic efforts to find biblical, or theological, generalities which will religiously dignify his promotional purposes. The will of God has got to be simplified into a push for the parish house. The Holy Spirit is reduced to a holy resource which can be used as a punch line for the enforcement of parish purposes. The theme of Christian obedience must be stripped of its judging ambiguities and forthwith used as a lever to secure commitment which is somehow necessarily correlated with observable services to the current and clamant program. The message, in short, is managed in terms of its instrumental usefulness for immediate goals."[3]

And with this meditation in mind we, the preaching successors to the country parson, go back to the classic textbooks on homiletics that we read in seminary and that —at least in some cases—inspired us to climb the steps of our first pulpit. But somehow the meditations recorded above interfere painfully and basically with the assumptions of the textbook writers. Of course, they contain beautiful insights into the high calling, but somehow they all seem to be more closely related to "that little parish church of which you can see the corner of a gable through the oaks which surround the churchyard" than to the place and situation in which we have to perform the "Christlike office" (Tertullian).

The sermon I was taught to preach had as its basic assumption that God also speaks today, and that he has chosen to address his people through the means of the world. In the sermon, the presence of Christ is established in the congregation; God speaks perceptibly in the sermon. In this human speech the Truth is revealed.[4] "Preaching is the Word of God which he himself has spoken; but he makes use, according to his good pleasure, of the ministry of a man who speaks to his fellowmen, in God's name, by means of a passage from Scripture."[5] It requires, says Barth, that a man is absolutely sure of his divine calling to preach: he must know that he could not do otherwise.[6] History without the preaching of law and gospel is an impenetrable chaos.[7]

And so the handbooks go on, depicting the preaching ministry in such semidivine terms and such cosmic dimensions that only the student (who does not yet have to preach on top of the other thousand tasks of his ministry), the genius (who can do all things at the same time), and the professors (whose position rightly allows them to sit back and study) really dare to understand what is said.

The question is, however, what about us, the ordinary people? The in-betweens, who are neither students any longer nor geniuses? Who are overworked men in a secularized society, living in the shadows of a mighty tradition but somehow aware that modern times are basically different from anything our predecessors experienced? To be sure, we preach. We have not gone on strike yet. We know that there is no substitute for telling the story again and again, and for telling it in the language and the situation in which we have grown up. We are, in Sittler's words, "exposed to and participate in the huge demolition and the tentative theological reconstruction of this twentieth century."[8]

That is where we stand, where we receive the impossible Word of God, and where we pass it on. We know that in one sense God's Word precedes us in the situation: he was there before we were, and the situation itself is not without the signs of his initiative. In another sense, the situation precedes the Word of God. We are in it before we can hear his voice and respond to it. We have no choice but to be in our own world, in which the invisible things command very little response, and in which man has become a substantially independent person, who does not only have a priest to intercede for him to an all-powerful God but who also has doctors, lawyers, scientists, and engineers to work out his appeal against nature and fate.

The metaphysical realities about which the Bible speaks—the Last Judgment, heaven and hell, the effects of prayer, angels and demons—have lost their self-evident authority and become very problematic. The theological questions for which people died a martyr's death—such as, How do I find a righteous God? or, Does the Spirit proceed from the Father and the Son or only from the

Father? or Did the miracles of the Old Testament and the New Testament really happen?—have lost their interest for most people, and we preach to people who want to know how to live, here and now. Ethical questions have replaced the theological ones, and lay problems have taken over from the theological issues. The old certainties in our congregations, so beautifully expressed in our traditional documents of faith, have become questionable to them and to us. The minister who knows everything is dead, and replaced by the minister who does everything but knows very little.

Together with our congregation we are caught in the frustration of the welfare society, in which the members are estranged from the powers who decide their fate and the final result of the production in which they are engaged. The world is a world of powers that are kept in a precarious balance by the experts and the managers.

Our strange predicament is that we are neither confident in it nor willing to yield any of its fruits. We are aware of the blistering criticism from the developing countries toward the "North" (Moscow/Washington) for not sharing our economic wealth, which to a large extent is built on the cheap labor and controlled markets of the "South" (Asia, Africa, Latin America). We are aware of the painful balance of power between so-called communist and so-called capitalist lands. We know about hunger and refugees, war and death. All these things are not farfetched, but fed into our living rooms by TV and press, and although hardly allowed to become vocal, they make up the subconsciousness of our culture. Fear, loneliness, frustration, rebellion, and extremism rise to the surface here and there when repression is no longer possible.

And in this world, we preach.

K. H. Miskotte, in a relatively old but still extremely gripping essay about preaching,[9] has said that we preach against the pagan and the Jew in us and around us.

The pagan in us and around us, he says, believes in life

and domesticates the revelation of grace into something like a feeling of life (*Lebensgefühl*); we become as confident about the rhythm of judgment and forgiveness as about the rhythm of the seasons. The crisis character of the kerygma is made into something that gives us confidence and becomes the fixed point that gives sense to life. The existing is worshiped. There is no terror and therefore no forgiveness.

The Jew in us and around us (in the congregation), who is, of course, in his deepest nature just as much a pagan as the rest of us, hurts our own piety, our belonging to the "right people," our being in possession of the proper prerequisite for having arrived.

In both cases, the uniqueness of the revelation to Israel is lost, and the sermon becomes an exhortation not to do anything that may distort the order in which we are, be it life itself or the right community. Preaching is, then, not communication anymore; it becomes wisdom or, in the best case, adoration.

But we know we have to do something else. We preach the unique revelation of God in Christ in our time, and we accept the challenge of the difference that makes. Karl Barth, in *Prayer and Preaching,* says, "Our preaching does not differ in essence from that of the prophets and apostles who 'saw and touched'; the difference is due to the different historical setting in which it takes place."[10] Some difference! That is exactly what the whole struggle in the church is all about: the only difference is the different historical setting! Many people in the church still engage in wishful thinking that the change is not too great, after all. Man has always been the same, they say. The church has survived the Turks, the Enlightenment, and the French Revolution, and it will also survive the technological and scientific era of rapid social change. Others, and I follow them, see such tremendous differences that we tend to agree with Karl Jaspers in his *Origin and Aim of History,*[11] where he says that European technology and science is utterly new for mankind. Greece and Asia did not produce it, but Europe did.

And those who feel that Jaspers is right, therefore, have to demand a renewal of all we think and do. And, therefore, our preaching needs careful appraisal as well.

1. What is there to say about preaching in a secularized society? My first remark is: Very little. I have two reasons for saying that. First of all, preaching is so strongly rooted in the church, as all the handbooks tell us, that all we say about homiletics depends on what we say about the church. Preaching in a house church, or with a Christian Aid team in Algeria, or in Coventry Cathedral, or in the East Berlin Lay Academy are very different things. There is not one doctrine of preaching that relates to all of them. Homiletics as a precise conception has followed the way of most well-defined conceptions; we have only perspective left!

And secondly, we have little to say because, in Bonhoeffer's words, we shall only know what we *do!* Since the church is only starting to become aware of what it is in a secularized society, we had better be careful about what we say!

Preaching, the classic method and the thousands of new attempts alike, has become an experiment. We only learn it while doing it. Therefore, we should put large question marks alongside all the methodological pages in the textbooks. Question marks on the page where the authors require penetrating scholarship: what about the scholarship of the apostles and what, for that matter, about the scholarship of 80 percent of our colleagues in the developing nations? Question marks at the plea for following a lectionary: what about a lectionary in a congregation where attendance changes each month? Question marks at the request for Biblical or topical preaching: how shall we decide for the pastor in Cuba or South Vietnam? Question marks at the ban on using other people's sermons: should not Martin Luther King's sermons or Probst

Grueber's meditations be reread rather than trying to improve on their inspired words?

2. Preaching in a secularized society can no longer be an individual task. I do not have to go through history again to show how through the ages preaching got more and more solidly into the hands of the priest and/or the theologian. With the great exceptions of Methodism and the Pentecostal tradition, in which the man spoke who was moved to speak, because he had something to contribute to all, the old tradition has been replaced by the sweating full-timer who, Sabbath after Sabbath, prepares his one or two sermons.

The Sunday service in my (Reformed) tradition is a one-man show, the excellence of which is measured either by the personal gifts of the preacher or by the never-enough-praised pious soul who can live on the experience of the physical presence of the brethren rather than on expositions that he needs for his spiritual breathing.

There has certainly been a tradition of counterargument against all this. Paul writes to the Ephesians, "To me, though I am the very least of all the saints, this grace was given, to preach to the Gentiles the unsearchable riches of Christ, and to make all men see what is the plan of the mystery hidden for ages in God who created all things; that *through the church* the manifold wisdom of God might now be made known to the principalities and powers in the heavenly places." (Eph. 3:8-10, RSV.) *The church* is making known: Paul's individual preaching is but a preparation for the church to be born. Then *this new community* will be engaged in the annunciation that has a cosmic character. The church addresses itself not only to its own members but to the supranatural powers that order and dominate our world!

In all the handbooks about preaching, a careful point is made about the church-centeredness of this ministry. Karl Barth reminds us of Luther's dictum, "There can be no Word of God apart from the people of God." And he himself adds, "Preaching has its place within the context of what is called the Church; it is bound up with the Church's existence and its mission."[12] However, in most theological minds, it was self-evident that the minister preaches. He must do it as a representative of the congregation, but he must do it. The old tradition, in which the man spoke who had something to say, is taken over by the tradition of the man who has to preach. In the Reformed tradition, the congregation becomes the judge of the sermon, the minister its executive.

When we were in seminary, we were told that the congregation was the bearer of the homiletic ministry, which it carried out by calling a man to do it for them; the congregation was the sounding board of the sermon, and therefore the preaching had to be done in a straight relationship to the visiting ministry; and the congregation was the addressee of the sermon.

Reading Bonhoeffer's *Works,* we find a curious mixture of the emphasis on the rather adolescent congregation, which simply has to listen, and attempts to escape from the individualistic method of sermon-writing. During the years of the church struggle, he tells his students over and over again "to come together and prepare their sermons together." With prayer "they should help each other to find the right words."[13]

It seems to me that we have to go one step farther and say that *the renewal of the preaching ministry is the rediscovery of its communal character.* Ever since the early church, Greek and Roman oratory has dominated the sermon. Not very long ago a homiletics class could hardly be distinguished from a rhetoric class. But if preaching is that unique combination of reminding each other of the story and of annunciation to the powers, the minister cannot preach alone. He needs a group of his people whose experience and questions should be the substance of the final product. Preaching is not Bible study but its result. In order to overcome both the somewhat professional and the highly individual efforts to communicate, we need to rediscover the communal and experiential approach.

Of course, every minister who has tried to have a sermon preparation group discovers how difficult this is. His well-ordered sermon structure goes out the window. He loses his reputation as a great preacher, and he probably does not fill his church to capacity. But then who told us that renewal was a way to a more glorious ministry and a fuller church? Sermon preparation groups are no educational gimmick; they belong to the nature of the church.

My experience has been that somehow the following method worked best. The congregation is split up into well-mixed groups of about fifteen people. These groups rotate the preaching ministry. Early in the week the group comes together with the minister. They listen to an exegesis of a passage, and meditate silently afterward for about half an hour. Then all share their insights and questions. Finally, a group decision is made on the most important questions. The preacher, either the minister or a layman, is responsible for the "final draft." Of course, he has the freedom to say that the group never came to the heart of the matter, but whether he agrees or disagrees, the voice of the whole congregation is heard on Sunday.

There is no reason why the final product should be performed by the minister. Many congregations are blessed with laymen much more vocal and gifted in communication than their ministers. What a blessing for the tired chief executive of the congregation if his contribution to the preaching preparation is mostly theological! He has to do the exegetical and doctrinal work, but he may be able to find somebody to do the final draft and the performance. Ministers who insist on preaching themselves may have to read a bit of psychology to start a healthy self-examination!

3. Maybe we have to say even more about the church-centeredness of the homiletic ministry. We have rediscovered during the last years that we have nothing but the Christian community to relate the faith to us and to remind us of the story. Very few people see visions or dream Old Testament dreams. The tradition of the gospel, in its outward forms, happens in a very secular way—from people to people. To check our doubts, to hear the Word of God, to make up our minds, to choose between the many possibilities given, we need each other. The church is made up of persons but distrusts individuals. We know that we finally have to make a personal decision about Jesus and all that his community stands for, but the process of decision-making is not an individual one. There, we live in restless communication with each other. Tillich has rightly said that only personalities can have community. The loss of personality is interdependent with the loss of community.[14] Individuals do not have community. They interrelate, but they have not yet matured into community personalities.

In the Victorian age, an individual may have been a strong, convinced man of principle. Secular man is other-directed. He needs his team and his community. His impulses come not in a vertical but in a horizontal way. The communally written sermon is, therefore, our response to a situation in which authority is not given to a person but is built up between persons. The individual preacher has no authority left (unless he is a charismatic or a genius, but they do not need to be made—they come!); he must earn it; it must be given to him by his hearers.

4. A sermon is not a chapter out of a systematic handbook: a sermon, especially today, is an encounter with *one* element of the revelation. It should, therefore, be *happily heretical;* it does not need to be balanced and secure on all sides. Preaching is the result of two efforts: the one to communicate, and the other to repeat. It is the tradition

being forced into the straitjacket of the new living language. For that reason, it seems to me, the New Testament records sermons that defy all exegetical method. In each sermon there is something of the extended incarnation— the Word of God becoming flesh. And as that is impossible, so is preaching impossible.

In my opinion there is nothing wrong in the often repeated observation that today ministers, and especially young ones, are so selective in their preaching. The humanity of Christ and the secular strands of the Old Testament, the absence of God and the power of man, are more popular than the divinity of Christ and the metaphysical trends in Scripture. But of course! As long as nobody makes a dogma out of this, there is no reason why one particular part of the Bible should not be more communicative than others. Let a generation preach about the humanity of Christ and, for the time being, do so in neglect of all other lines in Scripture. In sermons especially, communication may dominate the efforts to be complete.

5. In that same line, preaching in a secularized society can hardly be individualistic. Or, in the Bonhoeffer tradition, it cannot be religious: it cannot concentrate either on the metaphysical auxiliaries or on the desire for individual conversion. Preaching has to happen in nonreligious categories, i.e., in such a way that God's initiative for the whole world is seen and man finds his maturity, standing at God's side in the suffering of this world.

A sermon in the latter half of the twentieth century must be concrete and touch the problems that the people who are preparing it really have. It must aim squarely at social and political life and be written in a language that is really spoken. A sermon should be almost vulgar, as the Greek of the New Testament is almost vulgar.

6. Since we all say these days that secularization is a process of history which reveals God's work in history

and liberates man to the freedom in which he can choose, we must also insist that the sermon secularizes. The homiletic ministry is given to the church to unmask all controlling powers. A sermon should ridicule the ideologies. Remember that sermons are preached by the church to the powers.

The Dutch minister in the war who wore a Star of David on his gown (the danger sign obligatory for Jews in German-occupied nations) ridiculed the power of fascism, and that particular sermon hardly needed words. The Czech professor who preached what seemed an outrageously conservative sermon criticizing young people for their increasing moral misbehavior ridiculed the official ideology in which development toward Communism almost automatically increased moral excellence.

A sermon is not a comforting word; it builds up the congregation, it heightens the discernment of the community. It also comforts, not only the individual soul but the whole church, because it proclaims the Lordship of Christ and, consequently, the powerlessness of all other powers. The best sermons are often preached by God's unexpected preachers: the satirists and the comedians. I hold T.W.3 to be a powerful sermon on the British scene. They, much more than the minister, often teach people freedom to choose for or against life.

7. Finally, since we prepare our sermons together in this age, we have given up the great eloquent, rhetorical address. But since our God has a terrifying sense of humor, once in a while, he calls a man to behave in a very unchurchly way and to become a lonely, superb preacher. He is not in any sense the example on which we all have to model ourselves. He is an extraordinary gift to the church. God has produced them in Great Britain in quite some numbers. In our own day, perhaps none is greater than the American with the historical name, Martin Luther King.

We all preach our fumbling little sermonettes, so that

76   THE HUMILIATION OF THE CHURCH

a tradition may be safeguarded which offers platforms and pulpits to these men. What we perform inside, they shout from the rooftops. They are the signs of God's incredible patience with us. And they make the impossible ministry worthwhile.

NOTES

1. *The Recreations of a Country Parson,* first series, new edition (Longmans, Green & Co., London, 1876), p. 2.

2. *Ibid.,* p. 3.

3. Joseph Sittler, *The Ecology of Faith* (Muhlenberg Press, 1961), pp. 78–79.

4. See A. D. Müller, *Grundriss der Praktischen Theologie* (Bertelsmann Verlag, Gütersloh, 1950), pp. 159–210.

5. Karl Barth, *Prayer and Preaching* (SCM Press, Ltd., London, 1964), p. 65; published in part by The Westminster Press, 1963, under the title *The Preaching of the Gospel,* p. 9.

6. *Ibid.,* SCM Press ed., p. 83; The Westminster Press ed., p. 34.

7. H. Thielicke, "Die Christliche Botschaft an den Menschen des Säkularismus," in *Fragen des Christentums an die Moderne Welt* (J. C. B. Mohr, Tübingen, 1948), p. 220.

8. Sittler, *op. cit.,* p. 1.

9. K. H. Miskotte, *Het Waagstuk der Prediking* (Daamen, Den Haag, 1941).

10. Barth, *op. cit.,* SCM Press ed., p. 68; The Westminster Press ed., p. 14.

11. Jaspers, *Vom Ursprung und Ziel der Geschichte,* Part II, p. 82.

12. Barth, *op. cit.,* SCM Press ed., p. 73; The Westminster Press ed., p. 20.

13. Dietrich Bonhoeffer, *Gesammelte Schriften* (Chr. Kaiser Verlag, München, 1958). Quote from Vol. II, p. 440. See also Vol. III.

14. Paul Tillich, *The Protestant Era* (The University of Chicago Press, 1948), p. 264.

V

WORSHIP
IN A SECULARIZED WORLD

ONE OF THE MOST interesting phenomena of our decade is that all people talk about secularization, but very few really allow it to enter their religious practices. It seems that the process of secularization (by which we are gradually liberated from theological and metaphysical control) has a mainly descriptive function: when its story is told, everybody feels good; we have been recognized, we are explained to ourselves. No doubt this analytic process is always a means by which we are liberated, and that goes as much for Freud's probings into our inner selves as for Mannheim's insistence that it is mainly society which needs analysis. Secular analysis liberates. But it apparently also *makes inactive,* because the life of most student communities (and the church as a whole) continues as always: what happens in the lecture hall does not at all penetrate into the chapel.

We should be careful about hasty conclusions drawn from this observation; it may well be that the secularization theologians are merely playing, and that all our secular talk is only an intellectual game. Even if that is true, nothing is lost. Playing games is a way of proving freedom and a way of testing spirits. But at the same time, for many of our contemporaries, it was apparently no game, and they lost their faith during this process; the membership of most of our churches is decimated by it. Therefore, our game should be played well. In the theater, drama is not mere entertainment; it is a vicarious experiment in which the optimal involvement and necessary distance allow us to play a serious game in which we are involved and are given freedom.

It could, however, also be that there is so little relation between our secularization discussion groups and the prayer groups because we do not know how to *make* the connection. In that case, we are like most people involved in rapid change: we share the insights, but we do not have the tools and the practical know-how for what a modern day clearly expects of us.

Before we try to find the connection, we should warn each other that a renewed, adequate way of worshiping will not automatically fill our churches. Renewal is no gimmick to whistle back the Constantinian era. If we learn how to worship in a secularized world, it is because we have rediscovered obedience; we have heard anew the call to worship in our own society, and we obey the call as the people we happen to be.

Another word of warning: secularization is a word that describes a process[1] and therefore we cannot develop a static response to it. We are not looking for secularized liturgies that we want to substitute for the manuals of liturgies devised to survive through the ages, such as the *Missa Romana* or *The Book of Common Prayer*. Secularization may have reached a climax in Europe after the Second World War; we do not know what the next phase of the development may be. There is very little pointing in the direction of an American adventure of a religious boom, which in Europe would mean that people, for fear of an unknown future, would return to a presecularized era in which the churches would be filled again. But let nobody say it cannot happen.

There is also little to indicate that a new form of Christianity, diverse as our society and secular as the Bible, is arising out of the ruins of Christendom. That would be a sight worth seeing! A city without all these denominations: with one cathedral to celebrate the great festivals of the church's year, with an endless variety of teaching houses where people would learn again to live joyfully with their God; and around this cathedral and these teaching houses, people worshiping in their homes in the midst of the incredible mixture of interests and hopes and worries that each street harbors.

The most normal thing to expect seems the same as we have, but in an intensified form: more and more church buildings, functioning at best as the place where the ever-increasing numbers of tourists eat their lunch, the parishes slowly shrinking, the odd experiment providing food for those who can neither continue with the old nor disappear altogether.

Again, let no one say that these three possibilities are the only alternatives. The history of the Christian church is a series of very unexpected revolutions and renewals. In any case, it is not our business to worry about tomorrow: today's challenges suffice. The process of secularization has neither been stopped nor reached its fulfillment, nor indeed does its history so far make us expect a very predictable development.

A last word of warning: a Reformed chap from the Continent has trouble with worship in any case. The word is not translatable in current Dutch, nor German, nor French. Nor do the theologians of the day help us much. The first thing they tell us (and so it should be!) is that we have narrowed down the meaning of "worship" inexcusably by using it almost always for the solemn occasions on Sundays when the congregation assembles "for worship." The once existing and immediately relevant connection with the offering up of people's very selves (Rom. 12:1) and all they did, produced, thought, and lived has largely been floated away. Worship, like so many other things in life, like sex and politics, like eating and relaxing, has become an independent area of life. It can be very oppressive on Sundays: all these unknown people in their unusual clothes, listening in a very unfamiliar building to unfamiliar language. And especially when, usually only once in a very long while, one visits a congregation in real process of renewal—a group of people knowing each other, belonging, integrated, working away at new forms of liturgy, or indeed so familiar with their traditions that it is actualized in their using of it—the quality of the usual service of worship is unbearable.

There is a large group of people in the church who think that renewal of worship today represents a selling-out attitude toward the spirit of our time. Sometimes this remark is nothing but conservatism, but it can also be much more than that. The Orthodox churches, for instance, say that to us for deep reasons of theology and faith. The majestic liturgies of Chrysostom, James of Jerusalem, St. Mark, and St. Basil resisted the onslaught of the Arabs and Turks, the atheists and the Protestants—why should they not resist secularization as well? And we remember that for the Orthodox communities the holy liturgy is not only the order of worship used on Sundays, but confession, the Catechism, liturgy, and mission as well.

Protestants and even Roman Catholics, who are, after all, people of the West, should be very careful with the questions our Orthodox brethren raise. Of course, the young Orthodox Christian does not resist secularization any better than we do. The student in Athens is as confused as the student in London, and the Orthodox priest or theologian who does not see the need for the renewal of the church's life is simply reactionary. That is not the point. The point is that in the Eastern tradition, renewal will be mainly a renewal of the traditional liturgy. That requires experimentation: attempts to restore life and meaning to the elements of the liturgy, attempts to demand people's active participation in the central acts of the liturgy, attempts to restore the immediate relevance of the sermon, etc. Experimentation with traditional liturgies does not forbid Orthodoxy to experiment also with new forms of liturgy, but the new forms will be accidental, added to the central recital of the eternal drama.

We, whose minds work differently, should never try to walk with our heavy Western shoes through the rosebeds of the Eastern tradition. Maybe it is there that the tree, the leaves of which will heal the worship life of the nations, grows.

However, when someone in the churches of the Reformation (for whom liturgy has a quite different function) uses the same arguments, he should reread the account of the Continental and British reforms of the liturgy, in which the great divines paid tremendous attention to the need of the people of their time. Liturgical renewal in the days of the Reformation was the creation of new vessels to bring the old story to the people, and so to permit them to participate in it. It is that same courage, imagination, and love for the tradition, now in danger of once again being alienated from the people, that we need today. The need for a new Reformation is born from the call to hand over the old truths. If the renewal theologians of today were selling out to the spirit of the times, they would long since have followed the majority of their contemporaries and run away from the struggling community of faith.

The following remarks do not come from someone who has given up a meaningful participation in Christian worship, not even in the traditional ways. I am rooted firmly enough in Christian history to be able to draw meaning from what is also to me a foreign language, and I am sufficiently convinced of the necessity of the communal exercise of faith that what we usually do on Sundays remains meaningful, even if it is seriously questioned. I am, in other words, interested in "cleaning up." While waiting for the Reformation to come, I feel that many things can be done to make our worship more real and closer to the heart of our lives and our faith.

In the light of that position, I would like to make seven remarks. They are all related to the Bossey report on *The Meaning of the Secular*.[2]

1. A society in process of secularization is liberating itself from religious authority, perhaps from ontological authority in general; authority is not a given reality any longer but resides in relationships. A secular age, says Roger Mehl,[3] is an age of restless communication. Authority is established for the individual and for the community in a long process of reflection and discussion. Authoritative conclusions remain tentative. The conclusion does not stop the ongoing reflection. In order to be able to give authority to any conclusion or event, the recipient must have had some part in its establishment. That is true for parental authority and for intellectual authority, but also for spiritual authority. Experience of the truth is a *sine qua non* for acceptance of the truth. It seems that the early church knew about this already. Paul's letters to them are concerned with putting order into the rather chaotic participation of all participants in worship. But the order he proposes does not violate the essential communal and plural character of worship.

For us that means a radical departure from anything that has been called the one-man-show concept of worship. The service in which the minister (or, in conferences, the chaplain) *does* the worship while the congregation sits and listens corresponds to an outdated concept of authority and an unbiblical state of affairs. Sermon, prayers, and hymns used to be the work of the whole congregation, or at least of a group representing the congregation. The leader of the worship must be the man to whom people have really given the authority. He must have earned it. For the leader of our authentic worship, we need the same appointment as Ambrose received to be Bishop of Milan.

If our worship, our response to the living God, is not cast in terms of our age of restless communication, it will not be our worship at all. We have then chosen to join the worship of yesterday, but the Biblical "now" is neglected.

2. A society in process of secularization is characterized by a constant reexamination, by perpetual creative doubt through which all "given" elements are not only constantly reviewed but also appropriated. A secularized culture is always mobile—it changes, it experiments. The chief metaphor is that of *the way,* rather than *the family* or *the home.*

For our worship, this has many consequences. It helps us to understand the radical attack on the fixed place of worship that most of the renewal theologians are making. Church life, concentrated on an immensely stable building, is against their *Lebensgefühl* (feeling of life). I am sure that if the traditional liturgies of our time had been unmistakably chosen to be pilgrims' worship, concentrated on the moving character of God and his people, many people would find them much more relevant than the ones we have, and which are all promised-land liturgies in which the Temple in Jerusalem is more often used as standard allegory than either the Tabernacle or the wandering Ark.

If we want to worship in our day of creative doubt, we shall have to discover that the heart of our society beats in its experiments. Experimentally, we can come to an authentic expression of the Christian faith in an industrial and scientific society. If only the hymnologists would understand what they do to people by forcing them to sing out their faith in terms of nature! Look at our psalms and hymns! Not a word about cars, bridges, housing projects, motorways, or power plants. In the worship of the Christian church, modern civilization stands implicitly judged: it is not good enough to provide the metaphors of the liturgical language! We have more than enough books these days stressing the need for an urban expression of the faith,[4] but as long as it does not enter the worship life of the people, all our words are noncommittal. Sermons and educational materials are doomed when they clash with the liturgical practice of the community. A debate on an issue is a very different thing from singing a hymn about it!

So let us experiment. Let us write new hymns and work on prayers together. Let us celebrate the Blessed Sacrament in a hundred ways. Let us experiment with the old love feast, with or without the Sacrament in the middle. Let us baptize in rivers and in homes. Let us experiment with silence, that most unbearable part of Christian worship. Let us reconstruct the testimony to bring back the everyday life of the people into the worship where it belongs. And let us, above all, learn the heavenly gift bestowed upon Thomas, whose doubt did not stop until the Lord had appeared to him.

3. A world in process of secularization thinks functionally. The fascination with the ontological way of thinking (about what a thing *is*) has given way to a functional way of thinking (about what a thing *does*).[5] I am not prepared to make a case here for the Hebrew versus the Greek approaches to life, although quite a case could be made for the functional way in which the Hebrew mind works. Nor do I want to go into detail about the intricacies of the relation between the functional and the ontological approaches. Let us be satisfied with the remark that our time is more interested in the *functions* of being than in the *nature* of being. We are fascinated by what God has *done* and is *doing* in history, but whether he is omniscient, omnipotent, and omnipresent hardly makes us warm or cold. Biblical theology has shown us that we know God through his works and not through speculation or meditation. We worship the specific acts of God now and yesterday. Our God is the God of Abraham, Isaac, and Jacob, and not of the philosophers, as Pascal said, which is not a condemnation of the philosophers or their business, but an indication that God is known through obedience and not through the application of logic or speculation.

What does it mean to have a functional approach to worship? The negative implication is, I think, that we purify our language from all the ontological dust of the ages. We must learn again to use in prayer the simple (but not easy or naïve) language of the Lord's Prayer. All the words that ascribe to God unbiblical qualities of being which we today do not really understand, and which are fruits of theological speculation, should go. That is not to say that all old prayers should go. We would be amazed at how much functional language the traditional liturgies actually include. We need the courage both to test the old and to produce the new.

There is nothing functional about prayers of intercession that are not specific. To pray for the sick without saying (knowing?) who is sick is both a waste of energy and a blow to the sick. To pray for those in power without saying who is in power is making prayer a vehicle of hidden persuasion. To pray for the queen but not for her ministers is a sign of being about a hundred years behind the times. To send observers to the Vatican Council and not pray for the pope is *schizophrenia spiritualis*.

The same is true for the celebration of the Sacraments. A functional approach to the Sacraments includes some honest dealing both with the function of the elements and with the function of the whole event. I am in great sympathy with some of the more sectarian brethren[6] who abuse the churches for sprinkling rather than baptizing people. The Orthodox who bath the infant, and the Baptists who—in most of their churches—immerse the baptismal candidates, have something preciously functional to teach the churches here.

The same is true for the celebration of the Eucharist. The mysterious event at the altar rail needs a functional translation into the Biblical meal of the remembrance, presence, and fellowship of the Lord. How can we honestly criticize Rome for withholding the wine from the people when we give them wafers instead of bread? What have we done to the function of bread? We need both bread and wine, and we need to rediscover the meal. That makes the Eucharist in the first place a celebration of a small community—the house church and the conference congregation. In the big churches we may have to stylize the event, but we can do so meaningfully only when the participants have knowledge and experience of the real meal character of the eschatological celebration. Through the rediscovery of the agape, we may rediscover the Eucharist.

4. The theologians, after having overcome their initial fear of the phenomenon of secularization, have discovered that the Christian faith itself has a secularizing function.[7] Nothing liberates people from the control of powers and principalities more than the gospel itself. We now know that, without the preaching of the strange freedom in Christ, secularization in Europe would not have taken place; it is not accidental that secularization got hold of people in a Christianity-permeated culture.

The Christian faith secularizes in that it frees people from all other powers, so that man and his community can really decide whether they want this particular God or not, whether they want to go their own ways and to live independently, or whether they want to follow the way indicated and taken by the Messiah of Israel.

How does worship retain and rediscover its secularizing function? The attempt to find an answer to this question may be the most important thing we have to do. It speaks about the quality of all we do in worship.

If worship is to secularize the powers, it presupposes a keen knowledge of all those forces which try to enslave the congregation, be they political powers such as race or nationalism, economic powers such as the concentration on the exclusive furtherance of our own standard of living without an adequate politico-economic policy to abolish world economic injustice, or the cultural powers of the mass media with their subtle propaganda methods. The

sermon is, of course, the place where most of the discernment is done, but not only the sermon. If our prayers are
said to "hallow Thy name," they are also said to ridicule
and dethrone the other gods that try to solicit our worship.
In the confession of faith and the confession of sins, we do
not confess only general historical realities; we come to
grips with the actual society in which we live. Even if we
hold a concept of liturgy in which that event takes place
in the midst of the angels and in heaven rather than on
earth, we can still do nothing else but adore the Father,
Son, and Spirit, who are not remote from this world but
who engage in its history and who perform their actions in
the categories of time and space.

Real worship of God is as much a negation of all the
other gods as a relation to the one God we have decided
to follow. The ideologies of our time play in our worship
the negative counterpart of the confession of the truth in
Christ.[8]

5. As we said before, one of the negative aspects of
secularization is the departmentalizing of religion. The
sociologists speak of differentiation rather than secularization. They describe the process of continuous creation of
new structures and institutions to take over parts of the
earlier integrated functions of society and make them
entities in themselves. Religion, once the proud super-
structure of it all, controlling and dominating, and in the
best cases integrating all of life, tends to become more and
more a separate function, responsible for the metaphysical
department of man's life, his relation to God and the invisible world, and—on the human level—a well-defined
social community with the interrelations of the members
as its main characteristic.

This development has been one of the main reasons why
so many people have felt the church to be irrelevant to
their life and needs. It had little to do with the Monday-to-
Saturday routine, and did not contribute much to the in-

tegration of the consequences of faith and belonging to the third race into the struggles and frustrations of an authentic life.

For our worship, that means that we must see and structure our worship as an integrating force, bringing together all aspects of life under the sign of Christ and refashioning it in accord with what life in the Spirit means.

There are many experiments in the Christian community dealing with this aspect. The Protestant community of Taizé has, in its own way, fought for a new integration of life and worship through the total, lifelong commitment of the brothers; the community of Iona has done the same thing, combining social and political action with a rather elaborate worship life. But why cannot our parishes and conferences do the same thing? Why should we not bring into our services of worship the products of our hands— the factory-made articles, the books that have been written, and the newspapers that have been distributed? Why should not, in each service, a layman speak briefly about the area of life in which he is engaged? Should not the prayer of intercession always begin with some short, well-prepared introduction into the problem that the congregation wants to lift up to God?

One of the most impressive services of worship I have ever seen was in a Western European country with many political parties, in which a group of congregations came together during the election campaign to sing and pray, and to have their own members, engaged in different parties, simply and without propagandist motives explain why they voted for one party and not for another. Is that not worship? The reintegration of all life into our worship will probably be as painful a process as we have gone through while losing it all, but is it not worth it?

6. Cardinal Frings once wrote in the *Herder Korrespondenz* that tomorrow our worship will undoubtedly be much more sober and much more honest. Granted that this is probably true, how do we escape dullness? We have all

had the experience that when people start to worship in the categories of the modern age, they usually come up with something rather dull and unexciting. The great drama of Christian worship through the ages has been lost. Is that necessary? Can modern man be involved in tremendous mass drama in politics and culture, but not in his faith anymore? I do not believe it. Cardinal Frings may be right, but I hope that the church will also learn to experiment with the festive worship in which we use all our best imagination. The time for that is the great feasts. As Israel went up to Jerusalem for its great feast, so should the Christian church go up to its great festivals. And those days should indeed be the manifestation of the cosmic joy they represent.

I remember a Whitsunday service in the Domchurch in Utrecht, Holland. The Reformation certainly made something "honest and sober" out of that building, but ruined it in the process. But on this Whitsunday, all the Sunday school children of the town paraded through it, surrounding the austere Calvinists and their classic pews, playing on Biblical instruments—drums, tambourines, and flutes. And I am sure that the congregation got more of the joy of Pentecost out of the earsplitting music (?) those children made than out of whatever the preachers had to say that morning. The rediscovery of the joyful and festive character of worship is a necessary aspect of the renewal of worship life in the twentieth century.

7. Lastly, the process of secularization not only requires the renewal of the elements of the worship of the church; it also does things to the whole complex of the liturgy. The questions that we ask here are very preliminary and serve as a warning rather than as proposals. How easy it would be if all we had to do was to tidy up what the tradition had already left us!

All the above statements are made from the presupposition that "of course services of worship continue." It will always be Sunday again after the Sabbath has ended, and the churches will always manage to get a good number of the faithful to attend the service laid out for them.

But what if the rhythm of modern society is so different that the idea of the seven-day week disappears? Already the five-day working week has made quite a difference to the churches of Europe. Where people used to go to church on Sunday as their one and only involvement in the life of the church (and how many are there of this type?), it made quite a difference when the car was bought, and even more when that little weekend house somewhere out in no-man's-land was purchased. The weekend becomes "time away," not "time at home." The families who were involved in more church activities are suddenly without their Sunday worship or if they are going to church near their vacation house, live in two congregations at the same time.

When the rhythm of our life changes, our habits change. My grandfather read out of the Bible after the midday meal, but I take my midday meal in the office. My father read out of the Bible after the evening meal, but my evening meal is always too late to permit anything else afterward but hurrying the children to homework or bed. The Angelus no longer brings us to the daily prayer to the Virgin or to her Son; the days when the monks set the time for our worship is over. The pastor's family may keep it up vicariously for the whole community, but that makes him a rather special and lonely man.

What happens when Sunday disappears as the day of rest, as in some experiments in Eastern Europe? What if we do not get the necessary government permission to build churches anymore, so that the Sunday worshiper must know where the friends of Jesus gather? And what if such government order coincides with the new cottage in the country?

If all that happens, we will be brought back to that hurried little lunch together, once every few weeks, with the great silence in between—the silence which has already fallen over many a son of a devout worshiper and the cold shadows of which often reach our own hearts as well.

"And a great and strong wind rent the mountains, and brake in pieces the rocks before the Lord; but the Lord was not in the wind: and after the wind an earthquake; but the Lord was not in the earthquake: And after the earthquake a fire; but the Lord was not in the fire: and after the fire a still small voice. . . . And, behold, there came a voice unto him, and said, What doest thou here . . .?" (I Kings 19:11–13.)

NOTES

1. Cf. van Leeuwen, *Christianity in World History.*

2. *The Meaning of the Secular,* the report of a consultation at the Ecumenical Institute, Bossey, Geneva, compiled by Charles West, and obtainable from the World Student Christian Federation, P.B. 206, Geneva, in mimeographed form.

3. *Ibid.*

4. See Gibson Winter, *The New Creation as Metropolis* (The Macmillan Company, 1963); and Harvey Cox, *The Secular City.*

5. See the article by C. A. van Peursen in the "Secularization" issue of *Student World,* No. 1, 1963, published by World Student Christian Federation, Geneva.

6. "Sectarian" is used functionally here in the sense of isolating themselves, cutting themselves off from the others: *sectare* = cutting.

7. Van Leeuwen, *op. cit.*

8. Cf. Albert H. van den Heuvel, *These Rebellious Powers* (Friendship Press, 1965; SCM Press, Ltd., London, 1966).

VI

TOWARD A SECULAR UNDERSTANDING OF THE ECUMENICAL?

THE UNDERSTANDING OF THE ecumenical is once again changing. That is hardly a shocking statement to make about a movement, and only indicates that the thing is not yet dead. So let us rejoice in it and try to describe the development. We can do that only in a provisional way, and for this reason we are asking a question in the title rather than stating a definite fact, and we have also added some extra relativity with the word "Toward."

Much work has been done in describing the different connotations that the word "ecumenical" has had at different times and in different communities. The classical article about it is from W. A. Visser 't Hooft. He distinguishes at least seven different understandings of the same word:

"(a) pertaining to or representing the whole (inhabited) earth;

"(b) pertaining to or representing the whole of the (Roman) Empire;

"(c) pertaining to or representing the whole of the Church;

"(d) that which has universal ecclesiastical validity;

"(e) pertaining to the world-wide missionary outreach of the Church;

"(f) pertaining to the relations between and unity of

two or more Churches (or of Christians of various confessions);

"(*g*) that quality or attitude which expresses the consciousness of and desire for Christian unity."[1]

This article was written in the early nineteen fifties. Since then many new developments have taken place, but the clarity of the word has not become much greater. The word is still used for a great variety of events, things, and attitudes. Ecumenical tea parties, which denominational women's groups organize for each other, indicate that little more than restricted fellowship is sought with those who are of another denomination; ecumenical tourist offices offer trips to the Holy Land, using the word as an indication of the willingness of the management to organize non-denominational trips under the guidance of a minister; ecumenical institutes have been built, using the word to indicate that Visser 't Hooft's point g is being promoted, but also that common study and thinking are going on.

In the Netherlands a hot debate took place between those who called a joint appeal for funds to build new churches a highlight of ecumenicity and others who branded this action as a prostitution of the ecumenical movement.

There is a group of Christians who would only call those events and activities ecumenical which are related to the service of the church to the world: whether these events and activities involve people from more than one denomination is not important!

One community often uses the word in two slightly different ways: the Roman Catholic Church, gathered in an ecumenical council (point d), discusses the ecumenical movement (point f)! Since the beginning of the Vatican Council a discussion has been going on about whether the understanding of the ecumenical in the Roman Catholic Church is the same as that in the member churches of the World Council of Churches.[2] A member of the Central

Committee of the World Council of Churches wrote a lucid article about the three different understandings of the ecumenical as embodied in the Orthodox tradition, the Anglican/Protestant tradition, and the Roman Catholic Church.[3] So it has all become very difficult. Will the word "ecumenical" share the fate of so many other theological concepts, which—in the words of Flew—have died the death of a thousand qualifications?

It seems to me that in this semantic chaos there are three ways of understanding the ecumenical that are determining most of the thinking and activities of the ecumenical movement as it now stands (or moves!). It may be worthwhile to look in some detail at:

—the individual understanding of the ecumenical,
—the churchly understanding of the ecumenical,
—the secular understanding of the ecumenical.

Although I believe that the secular understanding of the ecumenical is the most recent (and the most promising!) attempt to express the tension of the unity that we have and the unity we seek, the other two are not to be despised and have not at all outlived their usefulness. On the contrary, they are very much with us and perform a useful and even necessary function in the life of the movement. But every generation has its own task in the ecumenical movement, and that task is so interwoven with the development of the society (or societies) in which we live, and on the other hand so directly related to the theological rediscoveries and finds of each new period, that emphases—and often whole concepts—are constantly changing.

One has only to mention a concept such as "mission" to see the obvious truth of such a statement.[4] The conceptualization of the faith is a never-ending attempt to catch in living language, in the koine of the day, what the fathers have believed and *in vain* tried to express sufficiently. The task of conceptualization is as much a historical as an existential activity. In it, tradition and obedience forge tools for actual communication.

The change of meaning that a word such as "ecumenical" undergoes should therefore not frighten but delight us, since it does not deny but accentuates the God of history we confess. When the use of a theological word becomes abused because it no longer communicates its living content, we should be keen to discern the stirrings of a new understanding that will always occur; for him who believes, it pinpoints the Spirit in our theological enterprise. The new understanding will be as inadequate as the previous one, though more useful; forgiveness and the desire to communicate are needed to overcome a feeling of despair in trying to say what can ultimately only be worshiped.

In the first John Knox lecture[5] just over ten years ago, Dr. Visser 't Hooft mentioned three main ways of understanding the ecumenical movement. The three catchwords he used were "Erasmian," "church-centered," and "pietist." Of the three, he felt that the Erasmian understanding had outlived its usefulness for several reasons. The Erasmian understanding of the ecumenical, he stated, is concerned with doctrine and order but in a very minimal way.

1. Church unity is possible and only possible on the basis of common agreement concerning a few and necessary and fundamental points of doctrine.

2. It follows, therefore, that the short creedal formulations of the early church are to be preferred, especially the Apostles' Creed, and new formulations concerning controversial points should be avoided. In all nonessentials, there should be great freedom; no attempt should be made to impose detailed confessions of faith.

Visser 't Hooft carefully says that the Erasmian simplification seemed to lead ultimately to a unity that would include all who believed in the Fatherhood of God and the brotherhood of all men, and that is hardly enough to do justice to the whole good news. He states that some of the Erasmian arguments have been incorporated in the actual ecumenical movement (we all know that what unites us is of decisive importance) but that others have been rejected (fundamental principles by themselves are not able to serve as a sufficiently strong basis for the one church of Christ). Therefore, he says, the Erasmian tradition in the understanding of the ecumenical has served its time and does not challenge us any longer.

There is much truth in this argument; the question, however, is whether Erasmus and his followers, such as Franciscus Junius, Hugo Grotius, and Jurien, or more recently Bishop Headlam and von Harnack, were not very close to yet another facet of the truth, which has hardly been taken up again. But we shall return to that later. It is true that the Erasmian understanding of the ecumenical—as traditionally conceived—no longer provides us with an alternative that is worth reviving.

For the generation that is now seriously involved in the ecumenical movement, the other two ways of understanding the ecumenical have also become problematic. Both the *individual* and the *churchly* understanding, as we experience them today, are unsatisfactory to many people.

The roots of the individual understanding of the ecumenical lay in the pietist movement,[6] that miraculous movement in the seventeenth and eighteenth centuries of church history in which the heart of the Christian religion was believed to lie not primarily in doctrine or order, but rather in its piety. The word "pietist" today is often used in a rather negative way, but we should never forget the glory of the period which revived the European churches that were suffering from the most deadly confessionalistic interpretation of the Reformation.

With roots in Holland and England, the movement got its name in Germany, where its best-known protagonists were also living. Both Spener, who demanded in his life (1635–1705) a reformation of piety rather than of order and doctrine, and Francke (1663–1727), the experimenter of pietistic ecumenism, were convinced that the unity of the church would be a grass-roots movement in which individual souls would have a consciousness of spiritual fellowship that in itself would be a manifestation of the ecumenical reality. Tersteegen, who did not—like many of the other Pietists—call organized religion "Babylon," kindly said that "everywhere souls can attain to the highest level of holiness and union with God" (and by "everywhere" he meant that this possibility was not even excluded from the churches). But Tersteegen was also convinced that, the church being invisible, "it is indifferent whether a man puts on this or that kind of religious clothing." Zinzendorf, whose life covered the first half of the eighteenth century, followed the same line: the unity of "all real Christians" belongs to his basic beliefs, but we must remember that union is not organizational—it is, in the first place, a union of hearts.

The individual understanding of the ecumenical has always given these pietist elements a place of honor. The participants in the ecumenical movement here are those who have discovered that there are Christians in the other churches as well. The goal of the ecumenical movement is the unity of the church through the reformation of the piety of the individual believers. Ecumenical education means education in the things that unite, rather than in the things that divide. There is a preference for the things we share: the Golden Rule, the simple gospel, the eternal truths, the common adoration and meditation on the life of Christ. The work camps, which are organized by those who live by the individual understanding of the ecumenical, are working on projects that are unrelated to the local churches, but simply organized to enrich the religious experience of the participants. The literature that is published by them stresses the value of being enriched by the piety of others.

There is a terrific sense of mission in the pietist movement—at least in the later developments: Zinzendorf has often been called the father of modern missions. The center of his pietism was not personal religiosity—although it easily became that—but Jesus Christ. It is for this reason that a closer study of the sources of the pietist movement impresses many of us today, because there is so much that binds us together: the doubts about organized religion; the growing insight that a reformation of doctrine and order are not enough and can be quite dead; the tremendously overpowering experience of unity in essentials that leaves the harsh, dividing realities pale and lifeless; and most of all its concentration on Jesus Christ. Visser 't Hooft is right when he says that the basic message of the pietist tradition always needs to be heard: renewal starts with *metanoia* and the message has to be shared with every man and proclaimed "in and out of season to all men in the world."

Pietism today seems to stand for sentimentality and emotionalism, for naïveté and otherworldliness—and there is reason for that because of many of the developments of the movement—but there is much more to it than that. Protestant Western European theology of the nineteenth century, with its emphasis on the religious experience of the individual, both accentuated and narrowed the insights of Pietism. The individualistic elements of Pietism were built up into a religion in which very little place was left for a confessing church. The most outstanding ecumenical creation of the nineteenth century, the Evangelical Alliance, was therefore not a movement of churches but "a voluntary union of individual Christians of different churches."[7]

On the other hand, the pietist tradition has given us unforgettable experiments in unity and renewal for which we should be grateful. The lay movements of the nineteenth century which came out of this tradition—the Y.M.C.A., Y.W.C.A., W.S.C.F.—have given us the leaders of the modern ecumenical movement. The awareness of its dangers should therefore not overshadow our gratefulness for the gifts received in that period. The dangers have been repeated so often that they hardly need mentioning: one-sided individualism, appearing in many pietist documents which hold that the basic reality in life is the soul's personal relation to God; ecleticism in ecumenism—we have unity with those to whom we feel akin. The individual understanding of the ecumenical almost always neglects the structures, not only of the church but also of the society in which the church is placed. The nineteenth-century church had more interest in culture than in social and economic structures.

For all its merits, modern people have a hard time with the individual understanding of the ecumenical. We have come to distrust our feelings and have learned how ineffective individual experience and action is if it does not take place in the context of the structures of a community. The rediscovery of the servant function of the church gives us guilty feelings about the egocentric character of much of the mysticism connected with popular pietism, and the emphasis on the necessary visibility of the body of Christ has overcome the subtle or crude statements about the invisible unity of the pious souls.

I am therefore sure that for many people the individual understanding of the ecumenical has also lost most of its challenge, and at best fulfills a role in the life of people who are exposed for the first time to the reality of the universality of the church of Christ and its calling in the world.

The churchly understanding of the ecumenical has a long and honorable history. Ever since there has been a church, there have been divisions, and ever since there have been divisions, there have also been movements to manifest the unity of the body of Christ—that unity which has been so clearly described in the Scriptures that any situation which confronts us with two or more communities confessing the same Christ but not in communion with each other deserves no other name than anomaly, blasphemy, and sin.

We can find witnesses to this in any century of the church's history. Let us take just three:

Clement of Alexandria writes: "It is my opinion, that the true church is one. . . . For from the very reason that God is one, and the Lord one, that which is in the highest degree honorable is lauded in consequence of its single-ness, being an imitation of the one first principle. In the nature of the One, then, is associated in a joint heritage the one Church, which they strive to cut asunder into many sects."

Cyprian is even more brutal in his accusation of divi-sions within the church. In his *De ecclesiae unitate* he holds that a martyr's death outside the church is stained by heresy and schism and cannot be washed clean by the blood shed for the Lord.

Many centuries later, Karl Barth says: "The plurality of the churches, of which we find no trace in the New Testa-ment, is in the light of the nature of the Church, of the Body of Christ, ontologically if you like, impossible. It is only possible as sin is possible."[8]

Every major father or doctor of the church—be it Augustine, Leo, Francis, Bernard, Hus, Luther, Calvin, Zwingli, Erasmus, Knox, Wesley, or whatever his name and nationality may be—has known that the church is one because the Lord is one, and that therefore a divided church betrays its origin and its calling.

But it took a long time before a common effort could be made that attempted the impossible by bringing all those communities which confessed the name of Jesus as Lord together into one ecclesia, whatever its form. Throughout the ages, individual Christians of different traditions have discovered that the Lord has not let his sheep in other folds starve, but it took nineteen cen-turies to come to a serious attempt to manifest the only possible conclusion of that discovery.

In the churchly understanding of the ecumenical, people stood for the manifestation of the unity in Christ by the historic confessions and by the dissenting communities that spring up in every century. Visser 't Hooft describes the churchly understanding of the ecumenical as follows:

"a. The design of God is to gather a people which is his own people and exists to glorify him. This Church of God, which is at the same time the Body of Christ, is by its very nature a single, united community. It follows that

"b. it is the task of the faithful to manifest that given unity in the world and that this unity

"c. is not the unity of the lowest common denominator, but rather that in which the faith is taught and believed in its wholeness and fullness."[9]

The churchly understanding of the ecumenical has been the mainstream of thought in the World Council of Churches from its beginning. Already the name distinguishes this organization from, for instance, the Evangelical Alliance. Here is no union of individual Christians, but a covenant of churches. The First Assembly did not hesitate to describe the ecumenical movement as a movement of churches:

"We pray for the churches' renewal as we pray for their unity. As Christ purifies us by His Spirit we shall find that we are drawn together and that there is no gain in unity unless it is unity in truth and holiness.

"We thank God for the ecumenical movement because we believe it is a movement in the direction which He wills. It has helped us to recognize our unity in Christ. We acknowledge that He is powerfully at work amongst us to lead us further to goals which we but dimly discern. We do not fully understand some of the things He has already done amongst us or their implications for our familiar ways. It is not always easy to reconcile our confessional and ecumenical loyalties. We also have much to gain from the encounter of the old-established Christian traditions with the vigorous, growing churches whose own traditions are still being formed. We bring these, and all other difficulties between us, into the World Council of Churches in order that we may steadily face them together. Because it is a Council of Churches, we must discuss them in a full sense of responsibility to those who send us, not pretending to agreements which our churches as a whole would repudiate.

"The World Council of Churches has come into existence because we have already recognized a responsibility to one another's churches in our Lord Jesus Christ. There is but one Lord and one Body. Therefore we cannot rest content with our present divisions."[10]

Churchly unity has since been the slogan of the Council. The Central Committee declared in 1951:

"It is important to insist that this word (ecumenical), which comes from the Greek word for the whole inhabited earth, is properly used to describe everything that relates to the whole task of the whole Church to bring the Gospel to the whole world. It therefore covers equally the missionary movement and the movement towards unity, and must not be used to describe the latter in contradistinction to the former."[11]

The debate on the unity we seek was provisionally summed up at New Delhi in a now-famous paragraph, which clearly envisages the unity of all in each place to such an extent that there is not only mutual recognition of ministry and doctrine, but also so much organizational unity that all can speak with one voice when the occasion requires:

"We believe that the unity which is both God's will and his gift to his Church is being made visible as all in each place who are baptized into Jesus Christ and confess him as Lord and Saviour are brought by the Holy Spirit into one fully committed fellowship, holding the one apostolic faith, preaching the one Gospel, breaking the one bread, joining in common prayer, and having a corporate life reaching out in witness and service to all and who at the same time are united with the whole Christian fellowship in all places and all ages in such wise that ministry and members are accepted by all, and that all can act and speak together as occasion requires for the tasks to which God calls his people."[12]

Whether this unity is best prepared by conciliar movements or by church negotiations is still an open question. The conciliar movement[13] is more inclined to concentrate on the local, national, and regional ecumenical councils, which would direct the work of a World Council, while the churchly understanding of the ecumenical has resulted in events and institutions that were directly representative of and responsible to the churches. It seems that the conciliar movement as it now stands hardly warrants such enthusiasm as it has provoked in earlier years.

As was said before, most of the ecumenical work now takes place within a churchly understanding. That means that the participants in the ecumenical movement are no longer interested individuals trying to enrich their personal piety, but delegated representatives of churches that have covenanted together. People may or may not be personally committed to the ecumenical movement—that is not the decisive thing; they must be able to represent their confession. The goal of the ecumenical movement now becomes the reunification of the historic confessions rather than the personal enrichment of the participants. The process by which this happens is a "fellowship in thought and action"[14] rather than a process in which people add up their spiritual insights.

Ecumenical education now includes the study of what divides us as well as what we have in common. It can be done only by people who are firmly rooted in the confession of their own denomination. Ecumenical youth work, therefore, is an encounter of well-trained young people under the guidance of well-trained chaplains. Churchly ecumenism produces large meetings in which the church

representatives discuss their historic agreements and dis-
agreements, and in which youth participants are allowed
to learn the language and the behavior of the ecumenical
movement. In this concept, work camps are organized
not, in the first place, to enrich the camp. The missionary
effort of the churches has to be integrated into the full
life and witness of the church. The intercommunion debate
is between two schools of theological thought in which
the commonly taken Eucharist is either the *telos* (goal)
or the *movens* (mover) of the unity movement. The
church is the center of attention, as the individual is the
center of attention for the pietist.

We do not have to say much about the merits of the
churchly understanding of the ecumenical: they are obvious. Not only did they create institutions through which
the churches could cooperate in political and social concerns, but the individualism of the earlier period has also
been overcome. Church union schemes were produced and
some churches even united. The Church of South India
not only has been a good example of what is possible if
Christians are willing to act on their commitments, but
also has strengthened the hope of thousands of people in
other churches who had almost given up their hope for
renewal and unity.

The churchly understanding of ecumenism has also
deeply affected theology: strong representatives of confessionality (Vilmos Vatja[15] distinguishes between a dangerous confessionalism and a salutary confessionality)
were forced to meet colleagues of different confessions;
ecumenical conferences inspired and (almost) forced
church leaders to take cognizance of other churches; and
almost all theologians today are engaged in a worldwide
systematic dialogue, whatever their own conviction about
the *oikoumene* may be.

But there is a growing feeling among many Christians
who are engaged in the ecumenical movement that something new is trying to break through: a new understanding

of the ecumenical that is the product of all these types mentioned above, but at the same time different from them all.

The reasons for its origins, first of all, have to do with the dissatisfaction with the last and strongest understanding of the ecumenical. Maybe we should say that the irritating by-products of the churchly understanding have pushed it into the open.

There is the ever-increasing danger of institutionalism[16] which tries to stifle the ecumenical movement with a misplaced loyalty to transistory positions and institutions. There is the doubt arising from the churchly representation which all too often fails to bring together the ecumenically committed and the creative theologians because they are often suspect in their own communities.[17] There is the doubt in the hearts of many people about denominational loyalty as a prerequisite to ecumenical participation;[18] there is the myth of confessional unity which is betrayed by the many different theological schools in all major traditions;[19] there is the danger of historicism which so often imprisons people in the past rather than liberates them for the future; there is the danger of Constantinianism which wants to build a larger church, to increase power and be a dam against Communism, Rome, or the world as such. And, most painful of all, there is the feeling that organic unity does not necessarily produce a more obedient church or a more effective tool in God's mission to the world.

These frustrations are nothing new. Ever since 1948, when the churches decided to make the ecumenical movement a movement of churches, people have warned against these dangers.[20] In the John Knox lecture of 1955 previously mentioned, Visser 't Hooft says that the church-centered approach and the pietist approach need each other to be fruitful. The call to conversion and the involvement of all churches, the need for personal commitment and the full attention for the complicated problems of faith and order, are all necessary. Many of us have the feeling, however, that the ecumenical movement has yielded yet another understanding that has not yet been fully explored but which makes itself heard more and more. For want of better words, I propose to call this *the secular understanding of the ecumenical.*

First of all, this represents a return to the original meaning of the word—pertaining to the whole (inhabited) earth, the known and cultivated world. The basic element of this understanding is that the ecumenical movement does not speak so much about the relations among the churches, but relations between the church and the world. Look at the following extract from a recent document of the World Student Christian Federation:

A. *The new ecumenical perspective*
The first major question, which is playing an increasingly important part in our ecumenical relationships, is concerned with the meaning of "the ecumenical." By this we mean the discovery which the churches participating in the ecumenical adventure are beginning to make: that the basic ecumenical concern is the relationship between the church and the world. The church is called to play a constructive role in the orders and structures of society, and, in the spirit of its Lord, to identify with mankind (Phil., ch. 2). For our Movements, this means an intensification of concern for the university in its radically secular character, for its humanization, and for its role in society as a potential centre of renewal. At the same time, it means less preoccupation with the denominations in the structures of our own Movements. The question of unity and the quest for renewal of the SCM structure are seen in a new perspective, determined by the mission of God to this world and our participation in it. This has important consequences for our Movements. . . . For all those who want to live out a faithful Christian presence in the university, the ecumenical issue acquires new meaning. No longer can the ecumenical dimension be mainly concerned with dialogue and co-operation between ecclesiastical or-

ganizations; it becomes the search for a form of authentic Christian presence which will not cut Christians off from the students with whom they share the basic struggle for a fuller life in the university, and which at the same time will allow them to be part of the whole body of Christ.[21]

In a way, this development could be expected, and is not even earthshakingly new. The modern ecumenical movement started with the individuals finding each other and struggling to find ways in which the unity they experienced could be manifested. Both their experience and their theological thinking made them concentrate on Christ and his church rather than on their own individual experiences. The missionary concern added momentum to this development. Concentrating on the church, however, meant rediscovering the world, since God called his church out of the world in order to serve it. The Christological concentration of modern theology also helped people to rediscover the church as a tool in the Messianic ministry that God performs in his world.

Neither can the rediscovery of the world as a basic theological concept be pinned down to one date or one theological school. It is the result of many themes concurring: the new and positive evaluation of secularization and therefore the positive evaluation of the end of the Constantinian era and its *corpus Christianum* theology; the upsurge of the behavioral sciences and sociology; the existentialist emphasis on the unprecedented newness of a technological society, the dialogue of churches producing a renewed interest in ecclesiology; the questioning that substituted an ontological approach (and no more than the approach) for a functional one.

It is also the work of the teachers of the church in this period of history, be it the logical next step of Barth's solid pointing to the incarnation, Tillich's correlation theory of theology and philosophy, Reinhold Niebuhr's apologetics, or the existentialist's emphasis on a theology whose task is, first of all, "to make the meaning of the proclamation of the Cross understandable to modern man in a language which he can understand."[22]

Within that gigantic task, the interest of many theologians has switched from the interest in a churchly understanding of the ecumenical to a secular one, of which the main characteristic is a search for ways in which the actual degree of common understanding and basic unity can function in provisional (not claiming to be the ultimate answer), vicarious (on behalf of the whole divided church) experiments of service and unity in the world. But this is still not enough. The world was not only rediscovered as the real addressee of the church and important as such; the world was also rediscovered as the object and the stage of God's active love and the place where he is at work through his risen Son and his Spirit, even before the church starts its work of mission and service to call man's attention to it. "The Church is taken into the victorious parade of the glorified Son of Man and on the way she notices that she is walking amidst the signs of the coming Kingdom."[23] Or, as it was said at New Delhi, "Christ is already the light of the world, of which he is Lord, and his light has preceded the bearers of the good news into the darkest places. The task of Christian witness is to point to him as the true light, which is already shining."[24]

The discovery that the church is not the only tool that God can or does use to work in his world, but is, rather, the announcer and celebrator of his work, has not yet fully been digested, but it has attracted the attention of many, especially younger, theologians. It has made them scouts for the footprints of the Master in the world, who conceive their primary task as discerning where signs of God's presence in the world can be seen, so that they may indeed celebrate them, point them out, and try to be faithful to them. The world has been rediscovered as the ring in which the victorious Wrestler challenges the powers and where he miraculously translates his apparent defeats into visible victory.

To them the churchly approach to the ecumenical looks like a dead alley in which the useless tool of a divided ecclesia is repaired in the wrong way: the only way to a renewed church is the common witness and service to the good news in the world. What is the use, they ask, of a united church that is not united in a real struggle for faithfulness in society? What does it help us to be united on doctrine and order if to the world we only look like a bigger and better ghetto? What is the use of a united liturgy if it does not spring fresh from a direct and common dialogue within the world in which we worship publicly? What is the use of a doctrinal consensus the theologians have sweated out if this common kerygma is not understood in the society where it is formulated? Or what is the use of an answer—which we proudly work out together—to a question that nobody in the world is asking? What is the use of a ministry accepted and recognized by all Christians if the ministers are not indeed engaged in the Messianic ministry to the world? For them the churchly understanding of the ecumenical, with all its apparent results and strength, takes place on a level where neither the terrific changes in society nor the degree of secularity in modern thinking have been taken seriously.

What, then, is the positive line the secular interpreters of the ecumenical are asking for? First of all, it seems to me, they agree with all engaged in the ecumenical movement that the real goal of the ecumenical movement is an authentic Christian community in each place. The New Delhi definition of the unity we seek is, therefore, very dear to them if properly understood. The authenticity, however, is not primarily determined by the fact that all who belong to the different denominations in that place are together, but by the fruits of those who are willing to engage themselves in the Messianic ministry of witness and service. Or, in other words, for them the participants in the ecumenical movement are *all those who care* and who are willing to test their faith in effective expressions of it. Whether those who care represent all historical traditions, or whether they are educated in the beliefs of their respective denominations, is secondary. Real Christian education—be it ecumenical or confessional—can only come when members of an authentic community test their traditions functionally in involvement. Ecumenical education for them is not the process of comparative ecclesiology, nor the creative discussion of theologians, but simply Christian education in the twentieth century—the exciting and frightening task of communal equipment for the missionary task. It is the process by which the Christians who care come together and work out "a confession in situation." Their different traditions play a functional role in this process. Those who are with them will be like "a householder, which bringeth forth out of his treasure things new and old" (Matt. 13:52).

Ecumenical education to them also means simply the necessary process of starting to reconceptualize the faith in terms of today. Anyone who has read a little bit of what the language analysts and their theological students tell us, knows that here a terrific field is still virtually virgin land.

If these people organize a work camp, the emphasis is not primarily on either participants or the local church, but on the project and its usefulness in the neighborhood where it takes place.

The secular understanding of the ecumenical matches anti-institutionalism with a great interest in adequate structures for the Christian community in the world.[25] These structures can be discovered only after careful consideration of what the society in which the gospel wants to be heard and lived demands in terms of effective service. Renewal of the structures of the church is, therefore, a process in which the best theological thinking—both traditional and creative—meets with an analysis of the actual stage in which each changing society finds itself.

It follows that in this type of thinking, the interest in national schemes of church unity gives way to a passion for local experiments of church renewal. This, of course, is also connected with the grave doubts many people have about the "renewability" of many (not all) local congregations as they exist at present. The tenacious resistance against renewal in our local churches and the complacency—if not plain conservatism—with which people cling to outdated and unaesthetic hymns, ununderstandable and unrelated prayers, and irrelevant sermons has made some of our most creative theologians and laymen cynical about even the possibility of rediscovering the local congregation,[26] this "dangerous experiment in the life of the Church."[27]

Ecumenical youth work all but disappears for those who have a secular understanding of the ecumenical. Once the question has been turned into a probing into the effective structures for a servant church, the generation issue changes with it. All concrete concerns that face the divided church face everyone and are new for everyone. Whether the Christian who struggles to find his place in a contribution to them is young or old is a secondary problem. Youth work, therefore, be it ecumenical or denominational, has as its primary objective bringing young and old together on the basis of their common concerns,[28] rather than taking the young people out of the whole of the church and teaching them in a corner. A certain amount of separate youth work may have to be done in those places where in society (and therefore in the church) the conflict between the generations cripples effective joint action. But youth work can never be done separately to such an extent that it gives the total community an excuse for creating experiments in unity and renewal among the young while the adult community sticks to its established ways. And let us remember that the locating of experiments in youth groups is not mainly bad because it produces a psychological barrier to later integration into the

life of the adult community (although it does!), but because the whole community needs to learn an experimental life again. Once again, these experiments for
wholeness between the generations can be discovered only
if we try them out. We will never know what we do not
do. (Bonhoeffer.)

Those who have a secular understanding of the ecumenical therefore believe that the road to unity is the local
street of experimentation that will eventually broaden into
a renewed national highway of Faith and Order. They do
not believe that there is an effective and legitimate short-
cut to this. It is possible to go from the streets onto the
highway, but not from the highway onto the streets. Or
in plain language: church union schemes follow local experimentation, and the fruits of the experiments are the
main theological contribution to the national theological
discussion; ecumenical experience is often more important
than ecumenical consensus, and precedents have proved to
be more persuasive than agreements. If national churches
unite without the local (and national) experiments of
unity, they simply produce a larger denomination, or they
produce a union but not unity. These unions may be
helpful because they give the renewal minorities an easier
structure in which to work together—but that is about all.
Church leaders and ecumenical officers should be sensitive
to the large group of people who work for church unity
with these and other motives, and whose concern for
truth is much more related to personal engagement in the
Messianic ministry than to conceptualized expressions of
agreement about the gospel. A bit more of the Erasmian
approach would not hurt the progress of the ecumenical
movement!

From the Erasmian tradition we learned to think about
a necessary minimum on the basis of which we can—and
should—start our experiments for fuller renewal and unity.
One of the trickier ecumenical problems is that of the
growth of unity or the problem of manifesting it. Until

now, the local manifestation was done either in church functions (prayer meetings, services, Bible-study groups) or in service groups, which had no churchly status at all. The secular understanding of the ecumenical pleads for the unity (not interaction!) of the two: experiments in being fully church together. The Erasmian tradition may give us the necessary minimum for this. But the Erasmian understanding only formulated the necessary presuppositions that gave us the possibilities for starting to work out together the detailed confession of faith that the experimental community of the faithful will have to make in each situation and in the language of the people they are working for and with. The Erasmian understanding lacks functionality but is still useful in providing major insights into the dynamics of the ecumenical movement.

From the individual understanding of the ecumenical we learned the need for conversion and personal commitment, as well as the emphasis on the *local* church. And most important was the stress on the missionary motivation of the ecumenical movement. Traditionally, however, the people coming to the ecumenical movement with this understanding do not have sufficient interest in the necessary visible structures for obedience and effective witness. They also lack the insight of the basic worldly concern of the ecumenical movement: God's beloved world, served by the Son and his friends in a Messianic ministry.

From the churchly understanding of the ecumenical, we learned the necessity of thinking in ecclesiological terms: it is not the souls who need unity; it is the body of Christ which is torn asunder that should be manifested in its uniqueness. We also learned from this understanding that we cannot be satisfied with a unity based on the lowest common denominator, but that we are responsible for the whole gospel preached to the whole world. However, the churchly understanding of the ecumenical has shown too little regard for the actual communities of the church, be they local, regional, or national. The grass roots are still not touched. It also lacks insight into the servant nature of the church, and did not show much interest in the radical newness of our age and the definite changes the world went through. It clung to historical thought patterns and made them determinative rather than preparatory for the future. It also showed little insight into the dynamic influences that modern thinking and modern life have had on traditional confessional beliefs, and tended to gloss over the disappearance of unity in any given confession.

Although the ecumenical movement—and certainly the World Council of Churches—is trying to keep the individual and the churchly understanding in balance, the result is not satisfying.

It is for this reason that people started to plead for a secular understanding of the ecumenical in which the concrete structures of society are taken seriously, and the challenge to restate the faith in the living language of today is accepted. It is a plea that a responsible risk is taken by allowing those who care to start—experimentally and vicariously—living out in concern-communities[29] the unity they have, which would help them discover a renewed confession, a renewed witness, a renewed service, and a renewed worship life on the spot.

Of course the dangers of this loom large. The biggest one is Pharisaism: We have done it, and all the others are backward and should die! This danger can be avoided only if the words "experimentally" and "vicariously" are rightly understood.

The second danger is isolationism. The universality of the church is not necessarily lost in concern-communities, but it is clear that it is only in communication with the church in other places and through a study of common problems in different situations that the body can make use of all its members.

A third problem is that the positive evaluation of the forces of secularization and the notion of the servant church may lead the concern-communities into a submission to the world, and that they thus become secularized rather than truly secular.

But these dangers are *only* dangers, and are by no means inevitable. And how could the gospel be lived if not in the face of the Tempter?

NOTES

1. W. A. Visser 't Hooft, "The Word 'Ecumenical' — Its History and Use," in *A History of the Ecumenical Movement, 1517–1948,* ed. by Ruth Rouse and Stephen Charles Neill (The Westminster Press, 1954, and S. P. C. K., London, 1954), pp. 735–740.

2. Much has been written about this; perhaps the easiest and most comprehensive article is a radio address by W. A. Visser 't Hooft, *Between Constantinople and Rome* (mimeographed, Information Department, World Council of Churches, 1964).

3. Hendrikus Berkhof, "Drie maal oecumenisch," in *Wending,* May, 1964.

4. Cf. *Mission und Oekumene* (München, 1963), *passim.*

5. "Our Ecumenical Task in the Light of History," published in *The Ecumenical Review,* July, 1955.

6. For the pietist tradition in the ecumenical movement, see Rouse and Neill, eds., *op. cit.,* pp. 82–93, 99–105, 309–333.

7. *Ibid.,* pp. 318–324.

8. Karl Barth, *Church Dogmatics,* Vol. IV, Part 1, tr. by G. W. Bromiley, p. 677 (The Doctrine of Reconciliation) (T. & T. Clark, Edinburgh, 1956; Charles Scribner's Sons, 1956).

9. W. A. Visser 't Hooft, in *The Ecumenical Review,* July, 1955.

10. Official Report of the First Assembly of the World Council of Churches, Amsterdam, 1948. Extract from the Report of Section I, *The Universal Church in God's Design.*

11. "The Calling of the Church to Mission and to Unity"; statement received by the Central Committee of the WCC at Rolle, Switzerland, 1951. See also Hendrikus Berkhof, "Oecumenische Kroniek" in *Wending* 18, p. 627: "In the meantime we should not forget that the word 'ecumenical' ought only to be used for what (*a*) is not carried by individuals but by churches, (*b*) is related to wrestling for the visible unity of these churches and (*c*) brings about co-operation between the churches in all kinds of practical fields."

12. *The New Delhi Report,* Report of the Section on Unity, paragraph 2 (SCM Press, Ltd., London, 1962), p. 116; *New Delhi Speaks* (SCM Press, Ltd., London, 1962), p. 55.

13. For a general introduction to the conciliar understanding of the process toward unity, cf. Henry P. Van Dusen, "The Significance of Conciliar Ecumenicity," *The Ecumenical Review,* Vol. XII (1959–1960), pp. 310 ff.

14. Statement received by Central Committee of the World Council of Churches at Toronto, 1950, on "The Church, the Churches, and the World Council of Churches."

15. Article entitled "Confessional Loyalty and Ecumenicity," *The Ecumenical Review,* Vol. XV, No. 1 (October, 1962).

16. *Institutionalism and Church Unity,* ed. by N. Ehrenstrom and W. G. Muelder (Association Press, 1963).

17. It is very interesting to see that the World Church and Society Conference prepared for 1966 came with a "revolutionary" proposal for attendance. In this scheme, great value is attached to the idea that mere representation is exchanged for expert attendance!

18. Cf. Minutes of the Faith and Order Commission meeting at St. Andrews, Scotland, 1960, p. 110: "3. The youth of the churches are troubled about the tension between the Ecumenical Movement and confessionalism. In many ways this tension forces youth into a posture of ecclesiastical schizophrenia. Many young people ask seriously, 'Do our churches really want us in ecumenical experiences?' . . . Other churches allow their youth the privilege of ecumenical encounter but always with confessional directives before, during, and after such conferences."

19. One reads this between the lines of Peter Brunner's

nostalgic contribution to *Das Bekenntnis im Leben der Kirche* (Berlin, 1963).

20. W. A. Visser 't Hooft, Opening Address to the Ecumenical Youth Assembly in Europe, Lausanne, 1960; printed in *Youth* Bulletin No. 2, p. 11 (World Council of Churches, Geneva). "And it is also a fact that the ecumenical movement of the churches is a battlefield where the forces of self-preservation and institutionalism are in conflict with the forces of renewal and advance."

21. W.S.C.F. document, "The Christian Community in the Academic World" (Geneva, 1965).

22. Rudolf Bultmann, *Glauben und Verstehen* (J. C. B. Mohr, Tübingen, 1962), Vol. III, p. 92.

23. Quotation is the translation of Mr. van den Heuvel from J. C. Hoekendijk, *De Kerk Binnenste Buiten* (Amsterdam, 1964), p. 24; American edition, translated by Isaac C. Rottenberg, *The Church Inside Out* (The Westminster Press, 1966), p. 24.

24. *The New Delhi Report,* Report of the Section on Witness, paragraph 1; *New Delhi Speaks,* p. 13.

25. The literature of the study on *The Missionary Structure of the Congregation* is edited by the Department on Studies in Evangelism, World Council of Churches. A good summary of the discussion appears in Colin Williams' books, *Where in the World?* and *What in the World?,* published by the Department on Evangelism of the National Council of the Churches of Christ in the U.S.A., New York.

26. Cf. Address by Pastor Ernst Lange to the Ecumenical Youth Assembly in Europe, Lausanne, 1960, "The Renewal Mission and Unity of the Local Church," *Youth* Bulletin No. 2, p. 55.

27. Theme of the 1965 annual Berlin Conference of the Ecumenical Section of the Youth Department of the EKiD.

28. Cf. Chapter IX in this book.

29. Cf. the writings of the Dutch physicist C. J. Dippel, particularly *Verkenning en Verwachting.*

VII

THE *HONEST TO GOD* DEBATE IN
ECUMENICAL PERSPECTIVE

THE LITTLE BOOK *Honest to God,* by J. A. T. Robinson,
the Anglican suffragan of Woolwich, and its companion
The Honest to God Debate have created such a stir in the
churches that one almost loses the courage to add another
article to the steady stream of (often emotional) writing.
However, since this debate immediately engaged members
of all churches in Great Britain,[1] and translations of the
book have appeared in seven languages, it may be fruitful
to look at the discussion from an ecumenical perspective.

It is in itself a small miracle that an English bishop
writes a book for college students, and that a year later
tens of thousands of Christians all over the globe are engaged in the same exercise as the public for whom the
book was written[2]: It shows the tremendous possibilities
both of the written word and of an idea brought forth at
the right time. It shows the vulnerability of our national
and denominational isolation too. No church today writes
only for its own audience; no country can isolate itself
any longer. Even if we are not ready for a worldwide
debate, we have to be prepared for it to happen.

The popularity of *Honest to God* is a complex thing. It
has to do with *kairos,* luck, and the most powerful means
of advertising, that of emotional, nervous critique. It certainly has to do with *kairos.* It was simply time for such a

book to appear. The theologians had kept their uncertainties away from the larger public for too long. The fact that a bishop would confess his doubts and (reluctantly) advocate a theological revolution was still shamefully new. For centuries the churches have specialized in answers and affirmations, and it seems to be very hard to come up to date with a society that presupposes an attitude of ceaseless questioning and creative doubt. At such a time the laity and a large part of the ministry were simply waiting for somebody to be "honest to God." The fact that it was a bishop increased the power of the event. Of course, the provocative, irritating, and sometimes unclear page of *The Observer*[3] also helped to sell the book, as did the flood of critical remarks from people who had not yet read the book but who "understood" from the newspaper reports what Robinson wanted to say. Both the nervous reaction of those who wanted the author excommunicated or at least deposed from his throne, and the quick welcome to their ranks given to the Bishop by some atheists, made people aware that something was at stake. So people bought the book: how many of them read it carefully is another question. Then the combination of the stir in the British churches, the very quick—and to my mind not very balanced—critique of some of the Bishop's superiors and colleagues made *Honest to God* a best seller. I believe, however, that the most important factor remains the kairotic one: the book came in time. That says more about the sensitiveness of the author than about the merits of the content: it tells even more about the people who bought it and reacted. For that reason, the letters written to Dr. Robinson and published in *The Debate* are some of the most important documents in the discussion. The book came in time, and not only in Great Britain; it also stirred up other countries. Germany deserves special mention. Even without an *Observer*-like publicity, and without an open debate in the church magazines, *Gott ist anders* sold extremely well. There can be but one conclusion. Whatever the theologians say and the churches think: these are the questions with which people wrestle.

The Book

The contents of the book are fairly simple. It was a book written for students and not for experts. Nowhere does the author imply that he is trying to write a standard work on theology (and he does not do this). His thesis is that the traditional language of faith, which uses mythological, supernatural, or religious symbols, is definitely out-of-date. The primitive projections of God with the related image of the triple-decker universe has had its day. We know God is not "up there," nor can we locate him somewhere "out there." The eternal Thou is only to be found in, with, and under the finite "thou." There we find God as the Depth and Ground of our being. Robinson does not say that the eternal Thou and the finite thou are identical. The rejection of supernaturalism is not an attack on transcendence and/or God. God is not *a* being or *a* person, but rather the Ground and Depth of all being, and personal as such.

In his chapter on Christology, Robinson follows Bonhoeffer's description of Jesus as "The Man for Others." Traditional Christology depicts Jesus as the Son of God who descended into this world and lived here as a migrant worker for thirty years, although he was in fact God. However, says the Bishop, Jesus never called himself God. He was a window through which we could see God at work. The life for others, as lived by Jesus, is the transcendence, because we meet God where ultimate love is given. The cross is the highest revelation of all this, and this love needs to be worked out by us in a style of living such as the world does not know.

In the practical chapters on liturgy, prayer, and the new morality, Robinson comes to the existential and central part of his book.

Liturgy is not an escape from the world, but an act in which we are reminded of the Ground of our being and where we are made aware of the presence of Christ in the others—the sick, the suffering, and the lonely.

Prayer was religiously understood as a retreat from the world into the presence of God. For Christians, prayer is an entry into the real meaning of the world. Prayer is opening oneself for God in one's life, and so for the Ground of one's being. Wrestling with others and with the complexity of their lives often brings more clarity than going away and bringing the others before God in prayer.

"The New Morality" is not a new set of ethical commandments, but is radical situational ethics, in which love is the only prescription. Robinson quotes extensively from Bultmann, Tillich, and Bonhoeffer, Wren-Lewis and Mac-Leod, trying to show up the common elements in their thinking, but choosing in the end for the depth language of Tillich as the most helpful of the three.

Both J. C. Hoekendijk[4] and M. Conway[5] have pleaded convincingly that the chapters of the book should be read in a different order from the one in which they are written. To really follow the argument, without getting bogged down by some rather careless writing in the beginning, the reader should start with the chapters on "Worldly Holiness" and " 'The New Morality.' " It is in these chapters that we find many reminiscences of Robinson's earlier and widely acclaimed writings. Here the author is at home and writes in an easy and convincing style. After these chapters, one should read the Christological background for the earlier argument (Ch. 4), and substantiate this with some of Robinson's earlier writings. Finally one can read Chs. 1, 2, and 7, which are rather sloppily written and hardly consistent. In other words, we should follow the author in his own logic and not necessarily in the way in which he has grouped his material. The second method may well help us to demolish the book quickly, but it will never make us understand the people who felt touched and helped by it. And they were met where they lived—often in a practical atheism in which all the articles of faith were correctly believed, but where the living God of the Bible had not taken charge of their lives. The book is written in the style of confessions rather than that of an intellectual treatise. The author does not write as a theologian, but as a normal man of the church. He does not write as an educator, a teacher, a critic, or an angry young man, but as a man who knows that he is engaged in the battle of the whole church to keep her faith in our modern society. We are all in that battle, and reading *Honest to God* as an expression of it will help us to evaluate it properly.

The Significance of the Debate for the Church

Before we speak about the theological significance of this debate, it is necessary to say a word about its significance for the church. It was clear from the first reactions which the book received that as many people were confused as were greatly helped by it. The Archbishop of Canterbury tried to speak the language of both groups and contributed congenially to the discussion in a tract[6] in which he treated the theological questions with considerable sympathy for Robinson's attempts, while he hit Robinson hard in his Presidential address to the Convocation of the Clergy. This combination indicates that the Primate thought the questions theologically in order, but pastorally dangerous. Other reactions betray a lack of understanding for the heterogeneity of our churches. Each Christian community includes a great many very different people. The time of the one-type Christian is over. We have moved into the modern pluriform society, and our churches show their involvement in this process in their pluriformity of membership. Not only do Christians not belong to one class or race, they also think and speak differently.

The people who were shocked were those to whom the old image of God "up there" did not present a problem. They were happy in the imagery of their youth, their parents, and their Sunday school. Robinson says that he is happy to leave them to those images, and that he wants to speak only to those who no longer feel that they can honestly go on using these terms. He knows that the one language of faith that is possible in a stable society is so no more, and he recognizes the various types of people coming together in his churches: those who are happy with traditional images, those who are unhappy with them but still stick to them, those who have gone through arguments and have mentally translated the old imagery, people who are lost in the language and climate of the Bible, and people who say so. They will all have their own language, but whether we can leave them to the traditional ways of thinking is to be questioned.

I would like to be more critical than that. We see daily in the east of Europe how church members are deeply troubled by childish atheism, attacking their faith on secondary questions of images and the consequences of scientific discoveries which in the theological field have long since stopped troubling the experts. But let us be clear: the theological victories over atheism have never really reached the laity. They have hardly permeated the preaching and teaching of the clergy, so that lip service is paid toward a new understanding of the message, but the way in which this new understanding is actualized often makes one doubt its reality. We should clearly say that all pastoral shielding of people from the new discoveries of our theology is dangerous. Of course, the teaching of modern discoveries in theology has to take place in love and wisdom, but it has to take place! Are we, the theologians, the only ones who are secularized? Is our faith so much stronger that we can bear what they cannot? The people who were shocked by Robinson's book were shocked in a timely way. If they have not thought about the consequences of living today, they have not thought enough. I cannot understand the argument that we have to be careful with the simple people and their faith. Of course we have to, but does that mean that we should hide from them what we know? Is it not much more a process of translation than a process of deciding what to say and what to keep back? The shock of the *Honest to God* debate is once again an indication of the predicament of our Christian education and religious instruction, and calls us urgently back to pastoral and theological honesty.

The second reaction to the book was that of people who thought it said nothing new: from the German professor who had not read the book but gladly aired his views on it and expressed his joy that "finally Great Britain had also seen the light," to the theologians who had gone through Bonhoeffer and Tillich and Bultmann before, and who in their naïveté assumed that these thoughts were now common property. They had apparently not seen that the readers of these theological exercises had been theologians, and that the debate was now suddenly passed on to the laity, for whom—we all agree—we study and write theology!

The third group, however, is the most interesting one. It is the group that was profoundly moved by *Honest to God;* the people who were liberated by it from a guilty conscience, who found a man—and a bishop at that—who was willing to be with them in their doubts and their confusion; who was willing to write a paperback before he had written a work in three volumes about it; who was willing to write in a very personal style, and who was even prepared to say on every other page that he was not sure he was right but that he wanted to communicate anyway. They met a man who was ready for a conversation, who was willing to exchange the robes of the teacher for the common clothes of a partner in the dialogue. They met a

man who was willing to write in contradictions and unfinished arguments without hiding and concealing.

It may be worthwhile to have a closer look at these
people. They are found on the fringe of the churches,
although very much in the center of the church. They are
not only theologians, and not all laymen. Some are young;
many are middle-aged or older. It is, therefore, not good
enough to make the response to Woolwich a generation
theme. No one church or one confession can claim them.
The Bishop of Woolwich has acted as a shepherd to
members of many churches, and that is in itself a significant, although not quite new, theological datum. It is a
group that includes many who had left the churches because they had not discovered a link between the secular
atmosphere in which they lived and the words of the
churches.

We should not delude ourselves about the questions the
laymen of today are asking. They are certainly not asking
for a little more responsibility in church affairs or for a
better rapport between pastor and congregation; they are
asking the most fundamental question of all: whether the
gospel makes sense in the secular world of 1966. What
they want is straight language in which the same courage
that they need in their own affairs sounds through. They
are not interested in renewal that brings the church a
bit more up to date; they ask for renewal as they know
it in the challenges put to the industries and scientific en-
terprises of our time. And that renewal is radical; it is
total. The response to *Honest to God* was so positive in
these quarters because it at least sounded radical. And
even if many people did not understand the implications
of what Robinson was saying, or indeed the argument he
was putting forward, it was their feelings, their mood, and
their temper that they heard expressed. Theologians may
have to learn to live with the fact that in our day and age
a correct and right statement has to be recognized before

it becomes true. Truth, in other words, is not an objective concept for most people in our age; it is relative. And as we all know from everyday experience, a clumsy argument from a man who understands and listens is better than the correct answer from somebody with whom we have no relationship.

The significance of the *Honest to God* debate for the churches is therefore connected, first, with the discovery of how many, how different, and how radical are the questions that are being asked. One statement of faith will satisfy and help only one of the many groups that inhabit our society. One set of morals will apply only to one section of the society in which we try to work out our relationships. One attempt to translate the gospel for modern man will communicate only to a few modern men. The same goes for liturgy, apostolate, service, theology, and church order. The time of the one form for all men is over. We must learn to live in and for a pluriform society. The quest for Christian unity—which is so close to the heart of the Revelation of the Triune God—gets another emphasis. Diversity gets the priority over unity because the problem lies in the many questions rather than in the common answer.

The second significant point is the gulf between lay thinking and theological thinking. In the course of the process of secularization, theology lost its relational character and became a science in itself. It developed its own laws and its own logic. It worked out a language and a philosophical terminology of its own. The churches insist that all members use this logic, this language, these systems, but today we sit uneasily on our heritages. Most ministers—overworked as they are—have little knowledge of the theology of their day, and they have to satisfy themselves with a spoonful of theological arguments that they pick up from more or less popular books on current theological trends. The expert theologians courageously go on producing, but the layman who wants and needs theological understanding of his ministry in the world is lost. He has neither the time nor the interest to engage in the conflicting theological systems; he has learned a long time ago that he should not look for answers in the church, but he still hopes that the churches can inspire him and give him a clue as to the direction in which his thinking has to lead.

Most laymen, however, have developed a language and a system of thinking in their own fields, and their ways of thinking have very little in common with the way in which the theological mind works. The layman has a different concept of authority, of doubt, of experience. He is inductively trained, whereas the theologian is deducing all the time. He is used to discussion in order to clarify, and meets theologians who discuss in order to answer; he is engaged in the most ferocious battles of competition, and gets sermons about love; he has to keep his position of careful balance, and is told to live like a child.

In other words, he belongs to two conflicting worlds. The conflict is there because the theological world speaks about him all the time in terms he does not understand. A theological discussion on what the laity is infuriates most laymen. The reason that some still keep coming is not interest in the theologian, but the fascination of the gospel, and the memory of the few times when it did indeed strike like lightning.

I think that all this is related to the *Honest to God* debate, or rather to its popularity. It is clear that thousands of laymen are ready to participate in the rethinking process that has to be done. But it will be a very different debate from what we (the theologians) expected. If the churches insist that their traditional theological categories are used, the debate will not even start. The discussion will have to be largely on the lines Robinson has sensed and laid out. Whether we can do better than his efforts will have to be demonstrated by somebody. In any case, the authors will have to be equally courageous in sharing all their thinking with the laity.

The *Honest to God* debate should also teach the churches how serious the call for total renewal is, or rather, how the apathy of the people in our churches, about which so many churchmen complain, is related to the "unrenewedness" of our communities. As soon as somebody speaks who is recognized and understood, the reaction is immediate.

The prospect of the renewal of the churches looked very good immediately after the war. There were many experiments, and a library was written about theological rediscoveries. We restored the Bible, the apostolate, the service, the unity, the laity, the younger generation to their proper places. We recognized the new situation of the world. We lived through the industrial, scientific, secularized managerial aspects of a world come of age. We rediscovered the teams, the house church, the servant church, the fraternal worker, the genuine experiment. The World Council of Churches appeared on the scene, and so did innumerable national and regional councils. We have industrial chaplaincies, lay academies, and ecumenical service institutions.

All this came into being in the churches. The time of the individual leaders of the ecumenical movement was gone; we greeted responsible churches in their place. The bookshelves where we kept our renewal books were known; people were inspired. Church leaders told their younger clergy to read the renewal literature and do something with it. But the renewal of the church to which the churches had pledged themselves, and about which all synods and bishops' councils spoke, did not come. Experiments remained experiments. The worlds where the church had not been present were analyzed and recognized, but not conquered. And the local church, more than any other expression of the church, remained the same—

a bit emptier perhaps, a bit redecorated perhaps, but it was not renewed.

And so the frustration grew. Many left; many still leave. The number of graduates of the theological schools who will not be ordained for the local ministry grows. The number of clergy who are queuing up for any secular job is indicative.

Of course we who are very much on the inside, we who live in the churches, and certainly we who—by a position in the World Council of Churches—see all the best experiments and know all the renewal men, can hardly feel like those who feel trapped in an unrenewed church. But we do not have to close our eyes to their situation. The frustration of some people about the renewal of the church is such that any book which blasts the old structure, each word that seems to be different from what has proved to be irrelevant to them, is welcomed. Much of the enthusiasm around *Honest to God* comes out of that desire for the total renewal of the church. Robinson may rightly have said that he was not radical enough, but with less than *Honest to God* we shall not get farther. And that is a lesson which we in the churches have not yet fully learned.

The Significance of the Debate for the Theology of Our Time

It is, in a way, unfair to require of a bishop that he should write brilliant theology. After all, bishops share the predicaments of all ordained men: they have to run institutions. They are shepherds with flocks that are too large, and they have responsibility for liturgical functions that are loudly questioned. Theology has become such a separate science that no man can master one of its fields any longer, and it cannot be expected that a Cambridge don become bishop could master all the fields.

Many theologians have said that Robinson has written a book which is theologically shallow, which does not take the questions raised seriously, and which, therefore, damages those who are engaged in the translation of the gospel to modern man. I agree that some of the chapters of *Honest to God* are sloppily written, but I am left with the question of the communicative writing. Is the revolution in theology a neat affair? Is it at all possible to popularize the thought of the great theologians of our day? Barth, Bultmann, Bonhoeffer, and Tillich have given us books of sermons that are readable for everybody (and everybody should read them!), but their methodological thought sits in heavy volumes on the shelves of libraries. Robinson went a step farther and popularized (made accessible to the people) their theories, or tried to. I am sure that this is very important. I am not so sure that the Bishop of Woolwich succeeded in being fully faithful to the theologians he quotes, but that is not the point here. Our theological experts have shown in their sermons that they have something meaningful to say. We now need to know their methods in order to cease being merely consumers of meaning. The fundamental question in the *Honest to God* debate is the question of the laity come of age. If the laymen are to be productive, vocal, meaningful members of the missionary church, they have to become partners of the theologians in the formulation, the sharpening, and the answering of the questions that need to be treated theologically. Laymen (like ordinary ministers who theologize in their leisure time) need tools, not finished products. The *Honest to God* debate has shown that we have not yet started that process, and that may be its most important contribution to theology today.

Having said this, we must look into the methods of relating the different theological schools that the Bishop employs. He gives the impression of being able to harmonize the interests of Bultmann and Bonhoeffer into something sounding very like Tillich in the end. The argument goes roughly like this: Tillich fights the supernatural, Bultmann fights the mythological, Bonhoeffer fights the religious, and all these fights are necessary. Therefore, they all fight at the same point.

The trouble with this argument, however, is that the warriors are not attacking together but are fighting each other. Tillich's philosophy of depth, in which the religious is a category that embraces the tragic and the mystic, is indeed very different from Bultmann's emphasis on the necessity of decision, conversion, and the will to believe. Bonhoeffer rejected them both, and said that, although Tillich was courageous in trying to interpret the evolution of the world in a religious sense, the world went on by itself. He agreed with Tillich that the world can be understood better than it understands itself, but that has to be done out of an understanding of the concrete and historical revelation of God rather than a philosophical understanding of the religious. Bonhoeffer saw the evolution of secularization as directly related to the work of Christ, and he rejected as historically outdated—and therefore fatal— the religious concepts through which he saw Tillich trying to save religion. Therefore, a choice has to be made between the Tillich and the Bonhoeffer approach to the modern world.

Bonhoeffer and Bultmann also form a very uncongenial combination. Bultmann's attempts to sift the mythological from the essence of the gospel are attacked by Bonhoeffer as methodologically impossible and conservative; the religious categories as such have to go. In both cases, Bonhoeffer holds that the others are not radical enough. Their attacks on traditional Christian belief do not go to the heart of the matter. Robinson recognizes this, but sticks basically with Tillich in his book, or at least he does so in the first two chapters.

On the other hand, we should not condemn Robinson too quickly for pasting together mutually exclusive points of view. We have to recognize that for each of us the school of thought where we feel most at home is not the only theology that is enlightening. The ecumenical movement is all about that—we are all enriched by theologians whose presuppositions we do not share. Especially in the field of renewal theology we discover many a friend traveling by another road. Those of us who are puzzled by the irrelevance of much theology, and whose integrity can only be kept by confessing that we know very little, have become very eclectic. We will listen to any theologian who recognizes that we have to start from scratch, and that a total renewal of the traditional categories in which we confessed our faith is called for. His basic presupposition is right, and even when many of his conclusions are wrong he is still "one of us." That element of truth has to be seen in Robinson's use of Tillich, Bonhoeffer, and Bultmann.

At the same time, I would agree with many voices in the discussion (Robinson's included) which have acknowledged that Bonhoeffer's letters are the most powerful expression of all this—most of all in their insistence on the combination of discipline and religionlessness. Bonhoeffer's concept of religion[7] keeps troubling many people. It is, however, quite simple. Religion is the perversion of faith. It is a combination of metaphysics and individualism. On the metaphysics side religion relies on a *deus ex machina,* God as stopgap, a working hypothesis that is used when man's powers fail. Individualism is correlated to metaphysics. Religion is interested in personal salvation; it is sublimated egotism, while faith is concerned with being for others, suffering with Christ in his world, and the wholeness of human existence.

Today the quest for a religionless approach seems to have become the excuse of those who have no discipline. Religionlessness is then taken to mean the absence of prayer, community life, and faith. A religionless approach to Christianity then merely ends in a plea for humanism, and theology is replaced by anthropology. Nobody should minimize the humanist movement, nor the necessity for a new anthropology, but the gospel cannot be reduced to that. Bonhoeffer was an aristocrat of discipline, a man with a performed life of prayer, meditation, and Bible study. He saw a type of man emerging who could hardly be told about this anymore, because he cannot function religiously. Among them, those who are called by Christ would have to practice their discipline in a hidden and silent way.

In his letters, Bonhoeffer speaks more about the non-Christian than about the Christian. The ecclesia will always have its discipline. There the story is known, the challenge answered, Christ joined in his pilgrimage through time and space. And, like Christ, the Christian will live *etsi Deus non daretur*. He will live the life of a mature man, not *quia Deus non daretur* but *as if* God did not exist, precisely because *God* wants him to live that way. There is little place here for Tillich's religious speculations because he is not interested in defending God or replacing God in the depth of our existence. His time is taken up by living as a simple man. Bonhoeffer was right insofar as the world showed no interest in Tillich's daring theories. Many Christians assailed in their traditional beliefs have learned much from him, and that is his power and reward. But the world ran farther along the path it had taken.

Many of Robinson's critics suggest—and I think rightly so—that it is not a question of replacing the images, but a matter of understanding why images are necessary, and how rich the Biblical message is in images which often transcend the primitive ones Robinson quotes. *Honest to God* may help many people to see that they have never grown up out of their Sunday school terminology, and that God for them is still "the old man in the sky." They discovered that they were indeed greatly troubled by the physical aspects of the ascension, the virgin birth, and the resurrection. Theologians—at least those who have graduated from this level of the problem—may laugh at that; they ought to understand that they have never really educated their people on those questions. Much work has still to be done on the image discussion. It would be fruitful to consider the many images of God's presence and absence in Biblical writing. It would then become clear that the very inconsistency of the Biblical images about God's location defeat most of Robinson's attack on the Biblical images as such.

Robinson knows that Tillich's image of Depth is not going to be helpful to people who do not want to engage in the real and basic challenge that the gospel (and all the Bible) presents when it speaks about the living God who challenges and speaks and corrects and comforts. We have discovered in the last decades that the Bible is not so much concerned with the being of God (and the *modi* of that being) but with the deeds of God, his relation to us and to his world. Of course, we can speak in too human a way about God, and Robinson is right in attacking that, but we can also speak too abstractly about God. If he becomes a principle, an idea, the ground of our being, have we not then substituted the god of the philosophers for the God of Abraham, Isaac, and Jacob?

Now, let nobody accuse *Honest to God* of having tried to do that. Robinson's book is far too human for that, too concerned with man in his relation to others. He writes far too deeply about prayer and love to be accused of the wish to curtail JHWH into a lifeless principle. My question is whether he does not in fact work *toward* it. The way in which the Bishop of Woolwich writes off the article of faith in God as *a* person seems to me to endanger a whole number of concepts that are vital to the Biblical witness. What happens to the concept of reconciliation when God is not a person, and Jesus is only the window onto the ground of our being? Does not prayer become meaningless when the addressee disappears? Does not faith become an attitude rather than a response? Does not history disappear in favor of an absurd chain of events that are circular or chaotic? What happens to the Biblical notion of the name in which God reveals himself as a person and through which he makes us individuals?

In Robinson's thinking, the term "God" has become a predicate used to indicate solidarity between men, but God lost his name and his history. I am not saying that the author *believes* that. He says repeatedly that he does not want to do it, and there is no reason to presuppose bad faith. I am merely backing up his critics who say that *in fact* he ends up with less than the living God of the gospel.

Not Wrong

But that, strangely enough, does not mean that Robinson is wrong. It merely means that he does not go far enough. What is said about prayer is beautiful, and I know of many people who were deeply moved by the chapter on "Worldly Holiness." But if we do not want to give up what is given to the church in the gospel, there is more to say. The revelation of the living God (Person and more than Person at the same time) allows *also* the retreat, the disengagement. The Man for Others shows that himself: he did not pray religiously, but he still knew what silence and disengagement were. Robinson is so much engaged in his battle against the wrong prayer that he tends to throw away the perfectly legitimate. The inconsistency of the book and the many self-contradictions in it are not a result of heresy, but the consequence of a desire to systematize. That to me seems the real weakness of *Honest to God*: it does not pay sufficient attention to the fragmentary nature of our actual understanding. In other words, Robinson still knows too much. He is not content with what he knows, and fills up the gaps with logical consequences, but this is just what we cannot do any longer. The people who were helped by this discussion were largely those who saw the wrong conclusions and who insisted on drawing consequences that went farther than the author wanted to go.

Many of Robinson's critics have reproached him for not paying more attention to Karl Barth in relation to his subject. Was not Barth the great initiator of the attack on religion? Did he not most forcibly attack natural theology with its normative moralism and metaphysics? Paul van Buren in his *The Secular Meaning of the Gospel* says that if the Bishop had taken his point of departure in Christology, he would have written a better book. Only if we proceed from God's self-disclosure in Christ shall we understand his nature and the essence of his dealings with man. Barth and, after all, Bonhoeffer (who remains a Barthian come of age) have opened our eyes to the covenant character of JHWH. Only in this light they come to understand the solidarity, the true humanity, and the commitment to this world. Interestingly enough, the conclusions to which Robinson comes are not very different, but he loses the confession of the Covenant God in trying to draw too many conclusions from his own point of departure. By not proceeding firmly from the incarnation of God—at least not in the composition of the book!—he reduces the theology to anthropology and loses God as a thou. His book would not have been *less* radical had he taken his beginnings in Christology; on the contrary, it would have been even more revolutionary.

The Ecumenical Significance of the Debate

We have to start all over again in our theological thinking. All sciences have gathered against the church and its message, and we must confess that our faith may be undaunted but our intellectual understanding of it has taken some severe blows. The historians have taught us that our traditions are less glorious and less factual than we believe.

The sociologists have explained to us in how earthly a manner we are organized; the natural scientists do not exactly expect help from us any longer; the language analysts dismiss our pronouncements; and the philosophers call us escapists. For a long time we thought that an intelligent explanation of our traditions would be sufficient for us to keep our intellectual integrity.

But some of us feel that more is called for. And that "more" will not be the business of the theologians alone. We shall have to learn to team up with representatives of other sciences; after all, we—the theologians—do not possess the truth. We share it with the whole church. The ecumenical significance of the *Honest to God* debate is to bring that to our minds again. Secondly, it has revealed to us how much the people are interested or, rather, how absolutely basic this is to them. Thirdly, we know that this process needs the widest participation from the church that we can ensure. Only in a mutual reinterpretation of our traditions can we take the next step. Confessional contributions will have to go through the sieve of the common understanding of all.

The Bishop of Woolwich has done us a great service in insisting on the missionary aspect of this colossal task. We have to do no more than testify to the hope that is in us.

NOTES

1. O. Fielding Clarke, *For Christ's Sake* (Morehouse-Barlow Co., 1963; The Religious Education Press, Ltd., Wallington, 1963); J. I. Packer, *Keep Yourselves from Idols* (Church Book Room Press, Ltd., London, 1963); Alan Richardson, ed., *Four Anchors from the Stern* (SCM Press, Ltd., London, 1963; Alec R. Allenson, Inc., 1963).

2. E.g., *Open Kaart*, Dutch reactions to *Honest to God* (*Wending*, 1963).

3. *The Observer*, March, 1963.

4. Cf. *Open Kaart*, O. C., pp. 681–692.

5. *Student World*, No. 3, 1963 (W.S.C.F.).

6. M. Ramsey, *Images Old and New* (S. P. C. K., London, 1963).

7. Clifford Green, "Bonhoeffer's Concept of Religion," *Union Seminary Quarterly Review*, November, 1963.

VIII

THE PUZZLE OF THE DOVE
AND THE SNAKE

"BEHOLD, I SEND YOU FORTH as sheep in the midst of wolves: be ye therefore wise as serpents, and harmless as doves." (Matt. 10:16.)

The editors of the *Student World* asked for an article that would describe the ethical situation of today, and readers may be interested to know that this is the third draft.

The first was one of those arrogant attempts to sum up the major theological arguments in the debate on Christian ethics. Since the author of this article is by no means an expert on the subject, the result looked as dull as the papers he used to write during his theological studies on subjects that in reality went far over his head. A little soul-searching quickly brought to mind the fact that the *Student World* people knew about my incompetence in the field, and therefore must have wanted something else from me. So I tore it up.

The second draft was so interesting (to myself) that I almost handed it in. It was an essay trying to analyze the actual situation of church and society and the threefold ethical dilemma of our time—the complexity of the situation, the absurdity of our predicament, and the loss of confidence in the ethical experts. It ended up (for a Presbyterian) dangerously close to Luther's two-realm theory, but that was not the reason for tearing up this draft as well. It went into the wastepaper basket because I discovered *ultimo tempore* that it was one of those unchecked exercises in modern Despair Theology, which finally seem to rest on presuppositions stolen from modern thinking and art forms rather than from one's own belief, however shaky that may be. That is not so bad as some people think. We all have to be true to the time in which God confronts us as well as to that story of the past that we have made the guide of our lives. The tension will therefore always exist, and indicate our nearness to the fire.

Let me expand that a bit. Most of us are rather frustrated in the churches. Certainly all those who have heard the proclamation about the renewal of the church, and know the irrelevance of much of what we are doing today in our cathedrals and chapels, have the feeling that we should worship, study, and act quite differently from the traditional way and with quite different people. Were we really sure about *what* should happen, the frustration would not be there: we would do it. But the uncertainty of how to get out of the ghetto of our denominations without hurting the mystery of the church creates the uncertainty. To say the same thing in other words: most of us are much more at home in the world than in that part of the world which is the domain of the traditional churches. Some of our leaders in the churches may think that we take the easy way out, and have simply conformed to the world. But is that true? We have discovered—thanks to many older prophets—that the world is the real battlefront where the struggle for the recognition of Christ goes on. There he is at work and calls us to him. We feel at home in the world because we often recognize Christ better there than in the churches. The struggle for social justice, the fight to overcome the lies of propaganda in politics, the battle for a balanced view of science, the attempts at a responsible life in the differentiated society in which we are placed have been shown to us as crises in which Jesus is very much present, and the churches—who taught us that—seem to have the greatest difficulty in keeping up with their own Lord in his shaping of history. The churches seem to resist the Lord more than the world, and because of that, we often fall into the pit of a despair theology which has given up not only the church but also the attempt to formulate an ethic that would be relevant for our age and that rests in the church. We are so discouraged that we would rather forget about all the big words and go out into the world and do something.

At the same time it is unfair to stop there. Even when the situation is such that we daily lose groups of our best laymen and theologians because they do not see how to manage the double loyalty (church/world), it must be said that during recent years a deeper insight into what God wants us to do has grown up. Biblical theology, sociology, and even modern systematics have helped us tremendously to clear out the old junk house of the nineteenth century (that is not to say that the nineteenth century did not need most of the things we now have to throw out!). The fact that most ethical pronouncements of the churches on the current crises of our age (race, sex, division of wealth, nuclear war, the quest for a just political system, etc.) are utterly irrelevant to many of us should not close our eyes to the tremendous help we have received from those theologians and laymen in the church who have courageously and almost miraculously kept the dove and the snake in the healthy and functional tension that the gospel provides for them.

There is no reason to bewail the stable society and its clear and severe morality if we prefer to live in our own exciting and bewildering age. There is no reason to weep about the endless process of secularization and the differentiation it brings to life, when we are happy about the freedom and the new insights of our age. The new freedom, brought by the process of secularization and wrested from the dominion of metaphysics and the way in which the church executed this dominion, demands a price. Let us pay it, then! There is no reason to be negative about our uncertainty in ethics as long as we still see so many new and exciting possible relations between the gospel we believe in and the challenges of a new era.

And let us thank God that he has humbled us into a new solidarity with all mankind. The worst mistake Christian ethics could make would be another attempt to distinguish the Christians from the rest of mankind, not only because people would laugh at us (that may be wholesome), not only because we have nothing very relevant to say about practical problems, but also because we may —for the first time in the history of the church—have the chance to live out what it means to be the firstfruits of a new creation. That asks at least for an optimal solidarity with groaning mankind as such. An independent Christian ethic is sectarian and foreign to the Bible. If our thinking about behavior and action is no contribution to the whole of our race, we betray what we are! When we try to trace God's action with his church, it may well be that in our shared confusion on ethics he reveals himself most clearly to us.

The Frustrations

In order to see our way out of the ethical dilemma (as far as possible) we should once again list briefly the different reasons why the old morality and even the old ethic broke down. The list is not complete and does not claim to be exhaustive; the reader can add his own elements. Clearly the situation is different in different continents, and I know that a Brazilian, a Ghanaian, and a Russian will be but little helped by my analysis. But it is also true that the European/North American frustrations are representative enough to be heard.

In the fourth paragraph of this article I mentioned three ethical problems. Maybe we should discuss these a bit.

First, there is the complexity of the situation. I remember a bad childhood experience. My uncle took me to a circus. There was the ice cream and the music, the clowns were unspeakably sad, and the horses almost too human to bear. But then came the jugglers. I still see the scene before my eyes. They started to throw bottles at each other. Three men throwing five bottles. Then six. Then seven. The bottles flew like knives through the air, but were caught and thrown on in a split second. It looked as if the mortality and sinfulness of man had been overcome. The man opposite the row where I was sitting looked sad. He had a clown's face and was older than the others. When the eighth bottle was introduced into the act, he failed, and in one moment the universe came to a halt. All seven bottles followed the first in what seemed to me like a thundering crash. The public roared. But the sad man's face did not change. He bowed and withdrew while his companions started to collect the rubbish.

That picture reminds me very much of our ethical situation. Ever since man emerged on the scene, responsible living has been an art of communal magic. We have always had neighbors, and without them no ethic would be of importance. Since we came into being, we have had to learn to juggle with bottles. And it required skill too— always. With the development of history, more and more bottles were introduced. The responsibilities were multiplied in accordance with the differentiation of life.

My great-grandfather had hardly any political responsibilities (except to protest), since democracy was not invented then. He had no problem with justice, since each crime listed was followed by a prescribed punishment. The complicated game of guilt and responsibility, played by judge, defense, psychiatrist, social worker, and criminal, had not yet been invented. He did not travel, and he worked where he slept and ate. He knew all the people around him and his behavior toward them. He did not know what it meant to play at least twenty parts a day. His society was stable, and so was his morality. If he transgressed the established morality, he did it in a stable way, and only served to stabilize the accepted morality.

But what about us? We vote. Our political responsibility requires knowledge of the political philosophies of our parties, the personality of our representatives, the situation in the world, and the predicament of the economy and social structure of our own land. In casting our vote we have to balance our responsibility for the help to less developed countries, housing in the next town, planning for the university of tomorrow, etc. We do not know much about many of these elements, but we vote nevertheless. If we are not politically minded, we are lost and vote in conformity with friends or family tradition, but in both cases we are frustrated. It is too complicated.

Life is not only politics. In our neighborhood we have migrant workers, and their predicament cries out for action. But I am too busy. I think about them at least three times a week when passing in my car on the way to my office, and that is it. When I got married, I swore not to live like my parents (who have a happy marriage!) and to be home at least during the weekends and one night a week. I broke my oath. Relatively well educated, I promised myself to keep up with theater, films, music, and reading once I was working. I broke my promise. Society has become very complex, and we have been made responsible for all things. We learn to live hastily, and we often resign in the face of the limited number of given responsibilities we really take seriously. Life has become so complex that it is very difficult to see whether our behavior in the larger context of world problems is responsible at all! What is so ethical about improving our national social security plans when we refuse to share our wealth with poorer nations? What right do we have to boast about our responsible society at home when we behave like animals abroad? A hundred years ago, the churches created totalitarianism in the now Communist countries by giving charity to the workers rather than the political rights for which they asked. To live in a differentiated society such as ours means to live in a structure in which social and political and cultural responsibilities are handed out in thousands of small shares. It means that nobody masters a field of knowledge by himself, and his actions, therefore, depend on confidence in an unknown number of experts, whose work we only know in a very simplified way. The responsibility of the individual is no longer connected with the knowledge he has about the actions he is responsible for.

But the complexity of the situation is not only connected with the quantity of the responsibilities each of us has today. Each issue in itself has become more complex because the knowledge we gather is so differentiated. The thief in the Middle Ages only had to acknowledge *what* he stole, and his punishment was in the book. Why, when, how, and where he did it was not important. A thief today may face a psychiatrist, some defense counsels, a minister, a few social workers, and a judge, and may get anything from a life term (psychiatric institution) to acquittal. Whether a man is guilty today depends on many more things than his confession of having done wrong. Subtle knowledge of the details of an action that is commonly called wrong may change my judgment from indignation to understanding to pity. Changing the context of a deed changes the judgment about it. Differentiation has come to us in the form of knowledge of other cultures where *our* crimes are expressions of normal conduct. Insight into the cultural determination of what is good and what is bad has done much to take away our faith in steady values and judgments.

All this does not necessarily lead to indifference or relativism in ethics. On the contrary, it may well lead us for the first time in history to a *free choice* between ethical possibilities. But it is clear that the old ethic, which was so much built on what a stable society had established as the things to do, does not hold for us. The stubborn defense of the traditional mind of the old pattern has done much to make us rebel and give up any attempt at responsible living in the new context of a secularized world.

Secondly, there is the absurdity of our predicament. Not very long ago I saw that masterly British satire, *Doctor Strangelove*. For two hours I and another five hundred co-creatures were reminded of the fact that we live in the shadow of the mushroom cloud. We laughed not because we were amused but because we did not know how to react. In the street, people were silent because they did not know what to say. The reaction in New York (where I saw the film) was confused. The authorities told the public in a firm voice that nobody needed to worry; no crazy general could start a nuclear war by himself! Only the President could do that, after counsel from a multitude of advisers. As if that were the point! Movie critics said that the film was sinister because this was not an issue to laugh about. But the point was well taken—man can start the annihilation of life, and we have no idea how to react to it. *How does responsible action look in the face of the absurd?* What is responsible action toward a rabid dog?

Most of us do not face up to the predicament of our age—at least not directly. We all have something in us of those Jews in Holland twenty-five years ago who until their last free minute could not believe that the Nazis would really arrest them and kill them. Perhaps one of my strongest feelings during *Doctor Strangelove* was that I felt uneasy about having to be reminded of our real situation. Modern art and mass media do more than we usually think to keep alive the knowledge of the absurdity of a situation in which, with our best minds and tools, we have developed the most destructive of all machines.

During the years when the letters and Gospels of the New Testament were written, the prevailing belief among the early Christians was that the end of the world was near. Their ethic was determined by that belief. The end of the age was anticipated with great expectation because Christians would share the glory of their coming Lord. A very high morality was kept on the basis of that promise; the prize was worth the greatest effort in the game. A certain otherworldliness seemed justified in the light of this. A certain withdrawal from the great complex questions of the Roman Empire in that day was the result. And why not? Why should Paul try to abolish the evil of slavery if the end of the world was drawing so near? Why bother about the division of wealth, the fate of the political prisoner, the relation between faith and politics, if the aeon was speeding toward its consummation?

Today a vague sense of secular eschatology has spread among the peoples of our time. It is not the Lord we are expecting, but the President pushing the notorious ultimate button. It is not the ascension into heaven with the other faithful that we hope for, but we have a faint feeling that the little pill from *On the Beach*[1] is closer to reality. This expectation of fear also has its repercussions in the field of ethics. Why bother? Why and how behave responsibly in an absurd age in which the responsibility of the political leaders does not inspire us with great confidence?

Thirdly, there is the loss of confidence in the ethical experts. There must have been a time in which a man, in good conscience, could pick up a book to see what he had to do in a certain situation. If old books on ethics are available to the reader, he should look at their indexes. Ethics were like homeopathy and etiquette: all necessary information on the right conduct was prescribed. Of course, if that time ever existed, it has now become history. No expert in Christian ethics will come with casuistic remarks. We have definitely learned that each new situation is unique and needs a decision of its own. So ethics have become the science of the guiding principles. When the engaged couple asks the minister whether they may sleep together before they are married, he will give them a sermon on respect for each other, love, the possible consequences, and the relation between marriage and the coitus. In easy cases, ethics still prescribe the answers; for the more difficult ones, we present the principles; but for the very difficult ones we cannot even do that.

The real trouble for the expert is the eternal struggle for the relation between continuity and radically new situations. Can the ethic of nuclear war be an updated ethic of traditional warfare? Is the ethic of work in an age of automation an updated doctrine of work on the farm? Is the ethical code for the metropolis an updated ethic of the small city and village? Most of the popular books on ethics give the feeling of minimizing the problem. The last chapter invariably gives answers and systematizes the questions. In a pastoral conversation, the first complaint of every man seeking advice is his disappointment with the experts he has read or heard.

In other words, the experts know too little and too much. First, too little: The problem today is so complex and has so many sides that each answer needs to consider many more—and many different—elements than the ethical expert can master. A quick judgment is seldom *recognized* as valid. Secondly, too much: When they come with answers and guiding principles, they often seem to ignore the real complexity of the question.

These are some of the frustrations we all deal with in relation to responsible decisions in our situation. The Christian here is not better or worse off than any other man. The problems are identical for all, and the loneliness of the man who makes his decisions himself without reference to another person or another reality is no bigger than the perplexity of the man who tries to make his decisions in the light of a Biblical ethic that was written under very different circumstances. The New Testament gives the Christian very little help in his secular life. It gives magnificent directions for the life of the church, and profound pictures of how to live with the brethren whom we acquired through the sacrifice of the Lord.

Both in the Sermon on the Mount and in the letter to the Romans, which are the most intense descriptions of the ethics of the early Christian community, the description is given of "life in the community of which God-in-Christ or Christ-with-God is the ever-present and ever-active source of all good, the constant director and inspirer, and in which men are members of each other."[2] The New Testament ethic is a koinonia ethic.[3] After some three hundred years in which the Christian church could safely live an independent life like a city on a hill, and after the following period in which the great experiment was tried of submitting the whole inhabited world to this community rule, we now face a new period in which neither road is open to us. God has opened our eyes too wide to his love for the world for us ever to be happy in a Christian ghetto. We have discovered that Jesus is Lord of history, we see his steps in the secular society, and we want to be there with him. We have discovered the nature of the church as a filling station or a hospital or a restaurant, but we live in the world.

The period of domination is also over. The world has liberated itself from the control of the church and from our koinonia ethics, which were always ill fitted for those who did not accept Jesus as God and Savior. So the situation is new; and we may as well be glad about it. The great experiment in which the church controlled the world with metaphysics, and *forced* people to love and have compassion, prostituted both the *agapē* and the *chesed* that the church proclaimed. It is impossible both to understand and to practice the Christian ethic without the *amor Dei,* or it does not make sense. For many centuries it did not. And because of its control function, the church itself could not function as it was called to do. The clarification of the situation of Christian ethics as basically a koinonia ethic is one of the fruits of the process of secularization.

This is not to say that with this clarification all problems for the church are solved. The structure of our churches is hardly encouraging for exercises in *agapē:* that requires small communities and more faith than many modern people can muster. Also *in* the church the problem of the new understanding of the gospel is pressing. But it can be said that at least the Biblical ethic provides a framework in which this can take place. A rediscovery of the communal character of the church and the ultimate defeat of individualism in our ranks could prepare us for a new attempt to rediscover the genius of the Christian cell.

But the real problem starts when we try to discover the relation between the Christian ethic we learned and received in the ecclesia *and* the solidarity with mankind in the struggle for human and responsible life.

Clearly that is no new problem. It is the one all Christians have struggled with ever since the Christian community was established. It is not necessary to survey here the whole gamut of possibilities of that relationship. Today the gap between believer and unbeliever is considerably smaller than it was yesterday, simply because both are confused. There is no clarity in either group. We both struggle with the same big questions, and we are both only guessing the answers. The gap is certainly smaller than it was before we learned from Jesus and his apostles that he himself unites the Christian and non-Christian in his Lordship over the world and his atonement for all. Therefore a double ethic—one for the world and one for the church—is as much out of the question as domination over the world or submission to it.

Then what is left to us? When our situation is complex in a way we never guessed before, ultimately absurd because of the threat of the annihilation of mankind, and when we have little confidence left in ethical experts, what shall we do?

Or what is being done? That is a not unimportant restatement of the question, because we all too often forget the wealth of helpful and relevant material that is offered to us these days.

First of all, let us not leave the question to the theologians. One of the most important discoveries of the last decades has been the ministry of the laity as the ministry of the church. Church is laity, we learned, and some of them are ordained for special tasks. The laity is not called to serve or help the ordained; they form the church. Therefore, they should also formulate the confession and the ethics of the community and its members. Without the practical knowledge of the laity who stand where the decisions are made, the church will not speak relevantly. The layman acts and reflects, and it is time that he took his rightful place in the formulation of our communal ethic as well. Whether the theologian does more than help him has to be found out in the process. Let the laymen take the initiative. Their first action should be a negative one. Let them frankly say what is relevant in the theologians' books and what is not, what is jargon and what is understandable. And let them insist that the ethical expert—who for some years to come will probably be an ordained man in most churches—work the problem through with them. The layman is an integral part of the personnel for the formulation of ethics. Usually he poses the problem, he collaborates with others in the church in the thinking through of the matter, and he is involved in the formulation of it all.

Secondly, we have to discover what ethical teamwork is, and we will learn that from a modern society. The more differentiated our society gets, the more specializations arise, the more expertise one single field of decisions requires, the more our society will have to rely on teamwork and partnership. H. Popitz[4] has shown that in a technological society like ours, people are related more intensely than ever, while at the same time there is more distance between individuals. Interdependence and loneliness are closely related. The only remedy against this interdependence-versus-mass-society structure is a freely accepted partnership that keeps both elements in a functional tension. Interdependence and loneliness are given factors; we do not have to create them. But we can choose whether we weld them into partnership or let them deteriorate into merely passively undergone unrelationships. For our way out of the ethical dilemma, this may be the most serious task. It is commonplace to say that our churches have lost the sense of partnership and team spirit that belongs so intrinsically to its nature. Most of our denominations are still voluntary organizations where people with the same convictions and the same feelings come to listen to the same minister. Only a radical transformation of these theater-churches into functional teams will help us discover both the koinonia of the church and a real sense of worship, which I take to be the gathering of the cells around the drama that celebrates the origin, sustainment, and hope of the ecclesia.

Partnership in ethics will put most things in their place. The theologian will be able to bring all his quiet study of the tradition, the Bible, and the contemporary philosophies to bear on the discussion; the people not involved in the situation will be able to think with the involved, and correct the emotions of the latter group; and the result of the team will be made known to others who have been working on their own questions. Liturgically the intercessions and the Eucharist will receive new meaning. In this way we may rediscover what confidence in the brethren can mean. Since everybody will be working on different questions, we may rediscover the exciting strength of the worship that brings us all together at the Table of the Lord, and we may finally have found the key to the complexity problem of present-day ethics.

Partnership is, moreover, the way to a rediscovery of a communal authority. Our society rests on creative doubt; that is the tool with which we made our scientific progress. It is the dominant ingredient of our school education; it is the governing principle of all scientific work. Doubt, whether creative or not, has become respectable in the course of the last centuries. It is only in the church that doubt remains a doubtful ingredient. Clearly the character of authority has changed with this development. It is no longer a given authority that comes with status or class. Authority has to be proved and proved again. It will always be doubted by those who have to recognize it. Von Oppen has rightly said that the tension of this age is related to the fact that people recognize at the same time the fundamental equality of all people and the need for recognized authority. Authority, therefore, has to be fought for. In practice this often means that the wrong people seize it and enforce it by illegitimate means. Only a society that is structured in teams and partnership will be able to overcome the authority problem.

The third element toward a positive understanding of our ethical situation is the rediscovery of the personal. Von Oppen in his *Das personale Zeitalter*[5] pleads forcefully for a recognition of the person as necessary for the functioning of society. Each modern society, he says, needs both the institutions, with their life and requirements, *and* the person to run, correct, abolish, and create them. The imaginative person, who can face the thing he is engaged in, the persons he is dealing with, and himself, is absolutely necessary for the functioning of our community. Von Oppen sees the gospel as a person-creating force, which—in the context of the congregation—never loses sight of man's personality.

In a way, that reinforces what we have said about partnership. We need to find a functional approach to the tension between individuality and partnership in order to overcome individualism and conformity. Both individualism and conformity are negative influences for decision-making. The individualist today is basically unable to master the complexity of the situation, while the conformist either will be unable to cope with the newness of the situation or will simply follow the majority behavior in his surroundings.

The church, far from being the only community that pretends to be able to produce persons, could, according to her nature, provide a useful service to society in that she does precisely this. Of course, we are once again speaking about the renewed church, in which that Biblical quality of person-in-community is being rediscovered and *worked out*. To avoid misunderstanding, we are not pleading for a renewal of the church so that we can serve society. Renewal works the other way around. Conversion that precedes, produces, and sustains renewal means a rediscovery of the nature of God's calling to be a servant community to the world. *Metanoia* can only be a recognition of our place in God's work in his world. The practical working out of service to the world is an indication of our willingness to hear the Word of God anew. We do not have enough space here to work out the implications of the attempt to concentrate on personality formation in the life of the church. It is the same thing as the plea for the formation of the whole church, laity and clergy alike. It includes all we have related to the lay academies and the study-group pattern. It also includes worship in which man is given a wholeness he can never discover anywhere else. It includes the silence of the retreat and the functional pilgrimage toward the places of renewal. It includes the constant presence of fraternal workers out of other cultures, which forbids us to speak about the others without the others being present, and so on.

I feel that the relation between worship and our ethical situation needs working out. All experts have pleaded for strong and convincing and factual counteraction against the despair that our absurd situation produces. Of course we all agree with that request. But fundamentally that demands a living out of a hope and certitude that we hardly know any longer. It needs more than an intellectual approach to the matter; it also needs more than a grim counteraction in politics. The Christian community has little else to offer the world here than the very heart of

her belief: the hope that it is exactly through absurdities—
"foolishness," as the Bible says (I Cor., chs. 1 and 2)—
that God saves his people. The way in which we express
that is our worship. The great liturgical traditions are better equipped here than the Protestants. If worship is
nothing but an order of service, there is little strength
against the power of despair and the absurd. I do not
think that we can do with less than something like the
liturgy of Chrysostom with its power. Let the Protestants
concentrate on their real strength: the sobriety of the
people of God around the table, breaking the bread, reading the Word, and instructing each other, while taking
care of those who are in need. They can indeed offer that
to the whole church as an intrinsic element in the life of
the koinonia. But let them learn from the Orthodox and
from the Roman Catholic (but from the Orthodox more
than from Rome) that all this simplicity is taken up in
something cosmic that wants to be expressed in nothing
less than apocalyptic-liturgical drama. The Revelation to
John is the Liturgy of the Absurd that needs further working out. In the light of our ethical predicament, the liturgical movement needs to renew both the dramatic and the
simple elements that have always accompanied the people
of God.

All I have done in these pages is to plead for a rediscovery of the church as a laboratory made available to the
society in which we stand; a place where, because of faith
and hope and love, there is more openness to the future
and more acceptance of the present if these three words
are lived and practiced and worked out in secular terms.

The Master has summed up the puzzle of the life of the
church—and therefore of the world—in terms of the snake
and the dove (Matt. 10:16). We have to live with the
devil and the Spirit. The pouring out of the Spirit does not
mean that we forget about the devil or that we kill him.
The power of the gospel is more daring than that: we use
the devil. We make friends with Mammon and we learn

to play with the Leviathan (Ps. 104:26). We work with chaos as much as we work with order. The tension between those two can be borne only if there is no ultimate danger in it, if the snake has lost his sting. We therefore need the promise of the secondary text with which the Gospel of Mark was read for many centuries: if they handle snakes, they will come to no harm (Mark 16:18).

NOTES

1. Nevil Shute, *On the Beach* (William Morrow & Company, Inc., Publishers, 1957; Signet Books, 1960).

2. Waldo Beach and H. R. Niebuhr, eds., *Christian Ethics* (The Ronald Press Co., 1955), p. 44.

3. See Lehmann, *Ethics in a Christian Context.*

4. H. Popitz, and others, *Techniek und Industriearbeit* (Tübingen, 1957).

5. D. von Oppen, *Das personale Zeitalter* (Kreuz Verlag, Stuttgart, 1960). See also D. von Oppen, "The Era of the Personal," in *Man in Community,* ed. by Egbert de Vries (Association Press, 1966; SCM Press, Ltd., London, 1966).

IX

YOUNG ADULTS
IN AN ADOLESCENT SOCIETY

I WAS ASKED TO SPEAK about the aims of an ecumenical ministry with young people. That means an invitation to speak about the aim of *all* church youth work going on in the churches that have covenanted together in national councils and in the World Council of Churches. It should not be necessary to defend that way of speaking—ecumenical work is always work of the church. Ecumenical youth work that has become independent from the life of the church is suspect by the very nature of the words. We, ecumenical youth workers, are not interested in extra youth work or different youth work but in renewal and unity of what our churches are already doing.

In a way, we know the aim of our youth work: it is to bring young people into a living relation with our Lord so that they will be mature Christians in the world. These words can be found in the written aims of most of our denominational youth departments. There are differences of emphasis, but no difference in essence. The trouble comes when we speak of the gap between our aim and the implementation of that aim, the gap between what we state we should do and what we are actually doing. *I do not think that I do an injustice to anybody when I observe that most of the youth work we do is determined by what attracts young people, what seems to prevent them from leaving our clubs and groups, and what slowly brings them*

into the life of our denominations as they are. The implementation of the aim of our youth work is limited by the
unwritten law that we have to produce church members
or keep our denomination as large as it is.

I sincerely hope that we have the courage—and also
sufficient distance from our own work in this safe conference center far away from our daily worries and troubles
—to discuss it with all openness, and I hope that together
we may advance in understanding and discernment.

The Young Generation and Our Youth Work

Different younger generations have different problems,
different questions, different needs, and different hopes.
Each generation is a new society, as a young person said
at one of our recent consultations.

We owe much to the work of H. H. Muchow,[1] who
describes the sociological analysis of youth as *epochal-
typisch,* as defining and describing the specific type of a
young generation in a given historical and cultural era.
Through a comparison of the attitudes and actions of
young people in the last days of the Greek and Roman
cultures with the attitudes of their counterparts before and
after 1770, 1813, and today, he proves his main thesis that
each cultural situation produces its own young generation
and, within that particular generation, attitudes and out-
looks peculiar to it.

At first sight, youth seems to be the same always. It is
easy to find quotations in writings of each age that speak
about young people in the same terms—Plato, Kant, and
Bertrand Russell have made almost identical remarks
about the new generation they saw grow up. Many people
have fallen into the temptation of concluding from these
similarities that young people are always the same. But
that is a dangerous conclusion. If young people were
always the same, adults could write off their criticism and
unrest without further ado. As a matter of fact, that is
what most adults do. "It belongs to youth to rebel," they

say, "but they will grow up one day and recognize the world for what it is. Young people have always been like that."

Muchow has successfully destroyed this somewhat careless argument and shown in his studies of the 1770 and 1813 generations that something unique can be found in each generation.

I think this insight may be useful for our discussions. Most of our youth work is in difficulties, and most of us are working with the same youth work philosophy and roughly the same methods—even when we have cleverly repainted and disguised them—as before the Great War. Our youth work is commonly built on the understanding that adults have ontological authority—that is, authority because of the fact that they *are* adults—and on the assumption that in social and ethical questions the experience of the adult is also valid for the young person, that the answers we found in our youth are still the same as the answers the young person should give today.

We believe it to be a valid thing that a whole generation is organized in groups and clubs; hence, we speak spitefully about the unreached and the unattached. In other words, we believe that we must emphasize the need for separate organizations for young people rather than work on socially inclusive groups.

We also believe—whatever we may say once in a while —that the intellectual activity of discussion and learning is more important than social and physical recreational exercises. I like Schelsky's suggestion that it is important to consider the fact that Eduard Spranger's book[2] on the psychology of young people has been reprinted twenty-six times since it was published in 1924. Spranger has taught us a lot, but his great weakness was that all his observations were made with regard to the upper-middle-class secondary school student. It is a fair guess that most of our youth work has been built on Spranger's leading idea that all youth is basically characterized by that special category. Maybe in his time that was true; indeed, the young worker tried to enter the habits and leisure-time activities of the upper class. Look at their pictures when they were dressed for the occasion—they looked like students. They played football—the sport of the rich at that time—and they bought walking sticks for the Sunday afternoon stroll, and their clothes were made in the style of the student group.

But it is interesting that Spranger did not have much use for the young workers and the young white-collar workers. He thought that they were underdeveloped students, people who, alas, could not afford to come up to standard. It took a long time before somebody started to take them seriously.

After the Second World War, a young Austrian wrote a book called *The Young Worker, A New Type*.[3] The most important word in that title is "type." In this publication, K. Bednarik fervently defended the thesis that in an industrial society the young worker necessarily becomes the type of the young. He—rather than the student—is now the expression of the image of society. He has money; he can therefore easily and seriously enter the market of the adult; he can consume and waste. The blue jeans, the motor scooter, the mass-produced music and literature, are created after his image of the young generation. So the young worker took over that position when the industrialized society took over from the Enlightenment and bourgeoisie. Bednarik's book is that of a prophet. It is romantic and written with a one-sided outlook. He was canonized in good German fashion ten years later by Helmut Schelsky in *The Skeptical Generation*.[4]

One of the interesting sidelines of the Schelsky study is that he can quote and use studies of American and British origin that clarify the position of the German generation he is describing—a powerful comment on how strong and how universal are the forces of a technological society. There are, of course, striking differences: The

British youngsters are not without the marks of their Commonwealth/Insular existence; the French cannot so quickly shake off the marks of their sovereignly maintained preindustrial *lycée* education; the Americans show the youth of their national history. But through that, and stronger than the differences, are the similarities between the young generations of countries that share the same technological developments.

When that generation is described, we youth workers feel uneasy, not only because most descriptions bring little encouragement for our organizations, but even more so because we only half recognize the youngsters who are described. We do recognize the picture, but somehow it does not seem to depict clearly the young people with whom we are working.

That could be an indication of a painful verdict: Are we working with a marginal group of youngsters, with the traditional minority, the obedient, the people who recognize our answers as valid for them—the answers we worked out a long time ago when society and its demands were very different? Are we working with a student-type youth work for a student-type youngster in the age of the worker-type younger generation? We should also consider the other side of the question: Is our failure to really connect with this young generation of today, which is the typological expression of society, due to the fact that we do not take seriously enough the fact that the world has changed rapidly since we ourselves were young?

We do not again need to draw up the description of the young generation; others have done that better. We remember quickly some titles that are descriptions in themselves: *The Skeptical Generation,* Germany; *The Vanishing Adolescent,* United States[5]; *Social Distrust of Youth,* France[6]; *The New Adults,* Holland.[7] There are hundreds of other books that try to depict the new generation, and although they may be conflicting in detail, their general outcome is very much alike. We see a generation that grows up in an industrial society, and the first impression they give is that *they are not young at all*.[8] They show the face of industrial man at large.

Let us stay a moment with this indication. First, "youth" is a very modern word. Children have always been there, children who could be taught, put to work, sold, who could play and grow up. But it was not until the eighteenth century that the adolescent was recognized as a person who had a right to form himself for the later task in life, who had problems of his own, who could be held responsible for many of his actions, but who did not yet play the role of an adult.

It is, therefore, also clear that youth work is a rather young phenomenon. Muchow sees it start with the German student groups in 1770. I would make a case for the middle of the nineteenth century, when the Y.M.C.A., the Y.W.C.A., and the teetotaler's movements started. In any case, it is only in the twentieth century that the adult-led youth organizations come into full swing. Youth as a separate phenomenon that makes itself clearly heard only comes into being when the values and the beliefs of an older generation do not hold good anymore. When society is stable and the experience of the adults is also valid for the adolescents, no youth work is needed—catechism classes, school, and playmates suffice. But when stable societies crumble, when the fathers have no experience in the questions the children are faced with, when yesterday's morals have become today's morality, when young people first have to ask the right questions and, subsequently, have to find the answers themselves because the answers they hear from their fathers seem irrelevant—in that case the younger generation gets a face of its own, a voice of its own, and a life of its own. It was precisely this process which prompted first the youth movements (in which adults played no part), and soon afterward necessitated the youth organizations, led by adults.

Now the sociologists tell us that youth is not young anymore. They are called young adults, semiadults, or simply new adults. They are not daring; they do not hate outrageously or love madly; there is no idealism (and we should not be too quick to call that an advantage). They are cool, detached, onlookers; they do not commit themselves. Whatever that means, it indicates that they have liberated themselves from the adults. We have no final, no ontological, authority over them. We cannot coerce them; we may threaten, implore, and beg, but we cannot coerce them or take them for granted. It has taken the young quite a long time to liberate themselves— for a long time authority was questioned but not disregarded; for a long time there was a fight between the generations. The observation that youth is not young anymore seems to be very important here. The industrial society does not regard difference in age as decisive; it looks at skill. It asks what a man can do and not how old he is; technological and industrial experience is often acquired in weeks rather than in years.

N. Beets, the Dutch juventologist, has seen a connection between this phenomenon and the popularity of the sports organizations. He says that because of the industrial powers in our society, people meet on the basis of capacity and not on the basis of age or experience. Young and old can meet, and do meet, without tension if no false ontological authority is assumed. In the world of sport, where team spirit is required to guide capacity, is found the best possibility for being together in a normal and existential way.

The second major characteristic of the young generation is that they are skeptical. The word *skeptische,* which was coined by Schelsky, may not be quite adequate; it may be too strong. Perhaps *Die nüchterne Generation* (the unsentimental, sober generation) would have been better. We all know what is meant by it. It stands for the attitude of an age group that has been hearing too many great theories, but has seen little progress. Even for this generation, which has no clear memories of the Great War, the down-to-earth atmosphere that dominated postwar thinking has had great influence.

The sober generation is also the most secularized generation that ever was (the next may be less or more secularized)—that is, more freed from metaphysical control than any living group before them. That means, in the words of George MacLeod during the Third British Conference of Christian Youth at Leicester, that they live by the inductive method—a thousand experiments with the same answer will provide an *ad hoc* truth. Great statements from which all truth is systematically deduced belong to an age that is over. Knowledge that cannot be verified, answers that may be correctly deduced from the presupposition of earlier authorities but that cannot be applied to their present situation, are suspect—or better, their relevance just escapes young people. In a discussion of religious experiences, Roessler reminds us that the difficulties of understanding between young and old often have their origin in the fact that the partners in that conversation speak from different worlds of experience. Many young people, therefore, complain about the unreal feelings adult statements give them, *although they recognize their sincerity.*

An industrial generation, caught in the revolution of a society that has to be restructured into an accepted pluralism, is growing stronger around us. Their task is one that is new. We profess that their essential need is the new life which has begun with the Master. Our aim is to make him known to them and to clarify his claims. That leads us to the following fundamental questions: How do we adjust, or how have we already adjusted, the implementation of the aim of our youth work to the new type of young people who have emerged in the industrial society? Do we indeed want "the new adult" to join organized youth work, or do we rejoice when he apparently does not need it? In other words, do we aim at large youth work,

or do we keep it as small as possible? How do we implement our aim with the skeptical or nonsentimental generation? What does the inductive method mean for our youth
work? Is Christian teaching always deductive? Do we have
examples of renewal in our youth work that are as fundamental as the changes in the attitudes of the young
generation?

Society and Our Youth Work

Our society has been described over the last years in
many ways. It has been called the Lonely Crowd, the
Personal Era (Germany), the Mobile Society. Words
such as "secularized," "mobile," "pluralistic," "deperson-
alized," "technological," "affluent," and "managerial" are
constantly in the air. Most of these words probably reveal
part of the truth of our community. Apparently, the adjustment of the new generation to society is not easy.
UNESCO studies on that topic have revealed the universal
nature of these integration troubles. The Teddy Boys, les
Blousons noirs, the Nozems, juvenile delinquents, and
Stilyagoy represent a worldwide phenomenon with names
in all languages of the world to classify them as the
maladjusted.

We are all caught up in the rapid social change of our
world. In Europe, the political developments toward a
greater degree of unity in the West and toward a deeper
cleavage between East and West put an extra burden on
the understanding of our place in the turmoil. I was once
greatly intrigued by Dr. Smirdall's outburst against the
Swedish approach to the Common Market. He said that
nobody could prove the economic advantage of that move,
but that it certainly contained a final blow to the tradition
of Swedish neutrality. Then came his main complaint:
everything was decided by the political experts and without the real knowledge of the people.

I think that is the predicament of most of us: everything is connected, and we feel left out of the decision-

making that goes on around us. The feeling of having little responsibility inevitably leads to being little involved. That is not to say that a younger generation is wholly negative about our civilization, because nobody really wants to live in any other era and so miss what our society offers to us—our technological equipment, our mass production, our means of transport (think of the ecumenical movement in 1700!), our communication, our growing freedom and interdependence at the same time. And although we pay a terrific price for what we have, we do not want to move back to poverty, ignorance, and quick death. The symbol of our technological society is the atom bomb, sign of human weakness, but we all prefer that terrifying symbol to the ones we have been able to cast off—the fortified city of the Middle Ages, the fasces as the symbol of unquestionable power, the coat of arms of the guilds as the symbol of fixed class structure, or the crude symbols of the primitive societies.

Our society is both frightening and exciting, and the adjustment of a new generation to it could not be easy. By "adjustment" I do not mean only the absence of revolt, but more the ability and freedom to contribute constructively and critically. In that respect, the maladjusted young people may be more adjusted than the majority of their contemporaries who do not worry and who fit the same description as most adults. Their first quest is for certainty, and their commitment to society comes late if it ever comes. Their fight seems to be for "more for ourselves," rather than for taking larger terms of reference.

The groups that are really having problems with our society seem to be small, but they are significant. On the one hand there is the group of Teddy Boys, or whatever they are called in your society—the ones who rebel without knowing exactly why. They make themselves heard, and that is all. They do not state their case; they are the case themselves. They rebel against the fictions on which our society is based; they see through the holy myths we have been building and the double-talk we are engaged in. They form one of the most interesting groups we have. Few of them last. The whole of society is after them, trying to integrate them, to help them, to condemn them. In short, we implore them to conform and to become as we are—to dress properly, to make less noise, to settle down, to join, to adjust. By the time they are thirty, most of them are saving for their car, playing with their children, and they shrug their shoulders at our funny elections and oratory. They smile rather sadly about their noisy past. That is one group.

The other group, which does not conform so easily, is the thinking crowd, the ones who want to know why, the people who are eligible for leadership, the future masters of the people.

But the large group conforms; they swallow the things they do not understand and they are silent. If we ask them what they think about the bomb, education, the under-developed countries, and the future of democracy, they shake their heads. They have joined the not-understood society as it is, and they hope that tomorrow will be better than today.

In his most interesting books, *The Noise of Solemn Assemblies* and *The Precarious Vision,*[9] Peter Berger has taught us that the churches have always been an integrating force in society. Or perhaps not always; it is said that there was a time in which the church had a disrupting voice, and we have even had some indications of that in recent decades. But, by and large, the churches have helped people to integrate into society. Churches are conservative, the sociologists tell us. In Russia, one of the major results of the existence of the churches under the Communist rule is that they have been an element of continuance, of durability, while everything else vanished.

Our youth work often does the same thing. In a few of the aims and functions of the youth work of our churches that were sent to me, it says that the adjustment of young people to our society is a major objective of the youth work we do. Sometimes it is called Civic Education, and then this word—which should stand for educating the individual to become a critical participant in society— is explained along straight conservative lines.

We all know the fight of the church against new forms of structure in society. We know that in the United States, Sunday morning is the most segregated hour of the week; we know that in Africa young people complain that the church does not help them a bit to prepare for the new society, since the church has essentially chosen the old forms. It is interesting to see that, initially, the gospel preached in Africa and Asia did not have that effect. In the course of our missions, whole societies were blown up and turned upside down. But as soon as the churches had their hold on society, they turned conservative and tried to integrate young people into society just as it was. Again the opposite examples are there, thanks be to God! But in general, the churches *are* an integrating factor.

And now, what does our youth work do in the society in which we live? I think it is a happy fact that we do at least talk about it. There have been times when even that did not happen, but now we talk. Whether we think that we should make all young people into Teddy Boys (revolting against society), or adjust all Teddy Boys to society as it is, we are busy with it. We say that young people should become interested in politics, that Christianity is worked out in social terms; we write about TV, modern dance, service overseas, refugees, democracy, and whatnot. In other words, we try to come to grips with the pluralistic society around us. But do we really help there? If I judge by the many youth magazines that come to my desk, I am afraid we do not. Are young people helped by a program that demonstrates the pluralism of our society by giving weekly articles about all the problems confronting us without ever having the time and the possibility of working out any one of these problems? Are we not frustrating them more by our endless insistence on new problems without ever going through the process of clearing up the underlying questions of living in a pluralistic society as such?

However, this cannot be the most important issue in the relationship of our youth work and the society around us. A much more basic issue is whether we prepare our young people for their participation in society in isolation from that society, or whether we prepare them for society by sending them into it. In youth work terms, do we organize our Christian youth separately or do we send them into secular youth organizations?

Until now, church youth work almost everywhere has tried to organize young people in church youth organizations. We did that not to isolate them from society, but to have a chance to prepare them for their role in society. In effect that meant that they were forced (or asked to choose) to organize in Christian rather than in secular organizations. They were too young, we said, to be already fully engaged in the world. Or we hoped that they would be engaged both in the world and in the church.

However, if Friedenberg, Schelsky, and others are right in saying that the youth of today are the new adults (in other words, *we* will not shelter them against anything), is it still right to try to establish as many Christian organizations as we can? And if that is right, what distinguishes them from all other youth organizations, since we ourselves apparently also have some difficulties in finding out what the mastering of the new society really means?

In the Lausanne youth conference in 1960, and ever since then, young Christians have asked for information on political and other social questions. I am afraid that was a naïve question. If we gave them that adequate information, they would drown in it. We, the leaders, cannot keep up with the thousands of problems that surround us; how could they? I am sure that there is a much more basic problem: What does adjustment to this new society really mean in terms of basic response? Is it eclecticism? Is it confidence in experts? Is it a struggle for more information?

Before I formulate some of these questions, there is one more thing to say. Is all this connected with our aim? Do we need to discuss the relation of youth work to the society in which we stand when we only want to bring young people into a living relationship with Christ? That question may sound funny, but the youth worker in all continents knows that this question is an eternal one. Not only in the more conservative circles, but even more so in our churches—everybody who has ever had to defend a budget for youth work in a synod or church conference will know what I mean!

The answer, then, is simple. Bringing young people into a living relation with Christ means bringing the whole person into contact with the Lord of the whole world. That means we cannot speak about young people without speaking about the society of which they are part. And we cannot speak about Christ without having to trace him in his world. My colleague in the World Council of Churches, C. I. Itty, constantly tells us about an Indian church where a cross stands before a window through which the world can be seen. On the cross it says, "I Am Not Here."

The questions here seem to be the following: How should our technological, pluralistic society function in our church youth work? What are our recent discoveries, and what are the areas we have not really covered? Is it right to organize Christian youth separately? What conception of the church is behind your answer to that question? Is our youth work an integrating factor into society, and should it be?

The Church and Our Youth Work

When speaking about the aims of youth work in the church, one has to make a decision right at the beginning. Should we speak about the church first and, after having tried to explain what the church is, then proceed to meditations about the younger generation in it? Or can we only speak about youth work in the church after first speaking about youth themselves and the society in which they are young and in which they have to come to grips with their faith and its community?

In choosing the second alternative, we have made an ecclesiological decision. We have, by the procedure we have followed, indicated that the form of the church and any special organization in it is an answer to God's call which comes to us *in* a specific situation. We have chosen for a servant church that is the incarnated Christ-in-community (as Bonhoeffer said) and against a dominating church that in its organization shows the world how to behave and how to live. And behind that decision lies the deeper one, which sees the Christ, King, Prophet, and Priest, as the servant of man, who took on the form of manhood and chose the lowly position of a slave.

Church youth work began when youth work itself began. In the nineteenth century, Christian youth organizations, led by young people, began when other youth organizations appeared. The Y.M.C.A., the Y.W.C.A., and the W.S.C.F. were Christian expressions of the same social phenomenon as the early German and French student groups. The young Christians responded with the same energy as their secular contemporaries did to the sleepy atmosphere of the bourgeosie of their days. Young people in society—and therefore in the church, which forms a part of society—went through a process of alienation from their parents and the leaders of their community. They no longer recognized the validity and authority of what was called normal and authoritative. The experience of the adults was neither inspiring nor normative for younger people, and so they felt compelled to organize themselves and to try to find their own answers. Youth requested the renewal of their community, and until they had been given a place to act responsibly, they withdrew from their elders and waited for their chance to take over.

The reactions of society and church were very similar. Rather than giving young people what they asked for, they copied the methods of the youth organizations, gave them adult leadership, and so created youth organizations that were in fact another channel of education through which society impressed itself on its young people.

This short historical survey does not do justice to the many splendid adult youth leaders who really joined the younger generation in its explorations; but the result was very much what has been called, in Continental science, the third milieu (next to the other two educational communities of family and school!).

A new period starts when the youth organizations all but disappear and youth work is done by adults either in direct liaison with the church or in independent organizations. This discussion, which has been livelier in the central European countries than in Great Britain or in Scandinavia, is still not resolved; both types still stand beside each other. The Christian organizations tended to say that they were the missionary arms of the church in the world or that they tried to help people to be Christian in the world by giving them community in it.

The church-organized, youth-organized people tend to say that there are at least two dangers in this theory—one of becoming an organization with its own historical traditions and principles, and the other of trying to take people out of society at large and so make them ghetto Christians. They would like to see the attention of the church for youth work express itself mainly through secular organizations, and keep the church for its proper functions of worship and Christian education. The place of the Christian is in the world; the church is only a place to be fed and to celebrate God's future.

I side heavily with the second group, and would indeed plead that the church give youth its proper place in its worship life, leadership, and teaching, but I do not see

why Christian youngsters should be organized for most
of their spare time in Christian youth work. If we do that,
we make Christians but not men. Becoming a Christian,
or growing in the Christian faith, can only take place in
the proper interrelation between the worshiping community and the community of all men. To be prepared for
Christian life can only be done while on the job of our
involvement with all people.

A new period started when large numbers of young
people stopped showing an interest in youth work led by
adults. This period, starting soon after the Second World
War, came about both because of the lack of interest in
what adults had to say and because of the enormous offers
of entertainment and recreation that the world made to a
younger generation. Society and youth work reacted to
this situation with two relatively new forms of youth work:
open youth work (in which the youth are given a place to
come together, and adults are offering to work out a program together with the participants) and new efforts of
leadership training to enable the community to really have
something to offer to interested young people. These two
new forms have had different measures of success in different countries. On the Continent, fewer young people
were attracted than in Great Britain, for instance. In
socialist countries there is often a certain pressure on
young people to join ideological youth organizations,
which have strong educational (and sometimes indoctri-
nating) overtones. Here again, the church followed the
general pattern of society and in many places offers the
same facilities as the state, with or without a direct Christian program attached to the different programs offered.

It is this development which puts many questions to
the churches. As long as the state does not provide any
facilities for a younger generation to meet and be on their
own, it is advisable that the church provide youth leaders
for open clubs and coffee bars, who are not only able to
help people discern their world but who are also able to

do so from the understanding of the community of faith. Youth leadership training, therefore, ought to emphasize the skill of real communication with the generation it tries to reach, as well as being able to look with their clubs for the relevance of the Christian faith in life. The less "integrated" the young people one works with are, the more difficult both sides of the task become.

Less self-evident to me are those methods which try to lure young people into a community with the ulterior motive of preaching the gospel to them. When this happens openly, and the youth club is advertised as a place where one is subjected to direct Christian missionary efforts, then there is nothing wrong. But when this happens in a hidden form, so that a dance is advertised but the real reason of the organizers is to get a sermon across, we use unworthy methods. They are unworthy for two reasons: we make the church look like an agent of the hidden persuaders, which has to steal sheep in order to grow, and we make Christians look dishonest because they advertise one thing and sell another. It also betrays the church as a community that is not interested in the free choice of people, but which tries to indoctrinate its visitors. We have a long way to go before our youth leaders discover the interest of the God of Israel in the whole person and his well-being, rather than His interest in their soul. And we also have a long way to go before we are restored to the Christian certitude that where we dare to present Christ through the simple, caring, and critical presence of his people, it is he himself who communicates the gospel to the others. Nothing is more deadly for the church amid a younger generation than to regard mission as an extra activity, which comes after and above the care for people. If our faith does not show in the way we are present with the young, defend them, discuss with them, and where necessary, help them, it is no faith, but a conviction or a set of principles.

It is, therefore, important to consider whether the church wants to carry on large organizations for youth work or whether it wants to prepare leaders for general and secular youth work. If our aim is to organize people into our churches or to proselytize people into the existing denominations, we should go ahead. If we are, however, interested in the young person himself and in his road to maturity, the Christian permeation of efforts by state and secular organizations is much more important.

The efforts to organize young people into our denominations are also hazardous because our denominations are so sick. All youth workers know about the awful problem of what to do with a pagan youngster who wants to become a Christian. We all know that faith excites community, and believing on one's own is in contradiction to what the documents of our faith teach; but the problem is, Does the community sustain the faith? I have many times personally seen young people come to faith but disappear again because of the unrenewed life of our churches. And I am sure that this is a general experience. If it were real faith, the person in question would all his life be an unhappy individual who found water to quench his thirst but no place where he could really drink it.

Here I think we reach the most crucial problem of church youth work, and the problem is not youth but our churches. Of course, there are the miraculous exceptions of people who do get integrated into our churches as they are, but let nobody think that such exceptions are to be expected. They are signs of God's humor rather than his vindication of our denominations!

The same problem occurs in the theology of mission, but with less vehemence. Walter Freytag used to stress from experience that God does not repeat churches in the mission fields but that he creates new ones. The repetition of Western churches in non-Western lands is abhorrent to any missionary activity these days. Is this only a valid statement for the faraway mission lands? Can we repeat a bourgeois church in industry? No, say Bishop Wickham and Dr. Wendland. Can we repeat a clergy church in an age of laity? No, say the Evangelical Academies. Can we then repeat an adult church in the youth culture of our day? But the answer is surely not a church for industry, a lay church, and a youth church. The answer must always be, a renewed church in which all the different groups in our society can live in the rhythm of unity and diversity; in which the liturgy, around Word and Table, unites what works so diversely in mission, service, and study.

A youth worker is, therefore, by the nature of his ministry, a person who becomes a living demand for renewal. A congregation that has not started on the road to renewal either repels or tames the young, but cannot make them live up to their unique calling in church and world. When the process of renewal has begun, the church can live in the tension of both inviting young people to take their place in the life and leadership on the road to renewal, and providing them with a place of their own where their contribution to the whole community can be worked out. An unrenewed church that boasts of having no trouble with its younger members is as heretical as a church that boasts of a large youth program which does not feed into the life and mission of the whole community.

And what about the unity of the church? All of you are quite aware of the mysterious perversions in the ecumenical movement by which all efforts seem to result in additional activities rather than uniting events. Ecumenical conferences come on top of denominational meetings; ecumenical literature has to be read—not instead of what exists but on top of it—and paragraphs on the ecumenical movement are even inserted in our instruction manuals after the chapter on church history.

Without wanting to be rude, I suggest that the everlasting existence of our denominational Christian education materials, summer camps, and leadership training is nothing more than an expression of fear for the consummation of unity. In the end, we do not want it, and we resist the leadership of our churches who at all large ecumenical conferences commit themselves and their churches to an obedience unto death (World Council of Churches Assembly, Evanston, 1954). I would like to believe otherwise and find some argument of allegiance to truth or conscience in all these separate organizations and activities, but I have not yet seen the unique character of any confessional approach to the questions of young people and sex, young people and peace, young people and poverty, young people and recreation, young people and politics—and still you all merrily keep publishing your little parochial brochures about it, missing both the chance to come up with something written by an expert (who will not write for one denomination, but might well do so for six), and to really present the Christian contribution on any question with the force of the whole Christian community.

Yes, somebody asks, but what about the matters of faith? All the subjects mentioned earlier were social. My reaction to that question, which is asked over and over again in the ecumenical struggle, is twofold. First of all, matters of faith that are not treated within a social and secular context are metaphysical speculations, and as such are secondary (although not unimportant) to the Christian faith and are very hard for a modern younger generation to understand. Secondly, where is the young leader who has not yet understood that in transmitting the (conflicting, contradicting, uneven, but glorious) Christian tradition to a younger generation, new concepts and a new language have to be used?

We have all spent hours in our denominational youth departments wrestling with the question of how to communicate the meaning of Baptism, of the Eucharist, of the Trinity, of atonement, of justification, of prayer, of conversion, to our youth groups. Some of us, with a bad conscience, have hammered the traditional explanations into their heads; and many of us, with an even worse conscience, have stopped speaking about it. Very few of us have tried to come to the heart of the matter in a new language, stammering, using heretical language perhaps, using oversimplifications always. And those of us who have tried have found that in this holy battle denominational barriers, which looked so formidable, become little higher than thresholds. On this battlefield we are all little Davids, to whom the heavy armor of Saul is little help, and we learn again to trust the pebble of faith in facing the blasphemous enemy.

Are not the questions here the following? How does the concept of the servant church influence our youth work? What are the methods by which we can train our leaders together? How can we come to a new form of experiment in which young people can experience being the church together? With whom and how do we discover a language of faith, intelligible for our time?

NOTES

1. H. H. Muchow, *Jugend und Zeitgeist* (Rowohltverlag, Hamburg, 1962).

2. Eduard Spranger, *Psychologie des Jugendalters* (Quelle & Meyer, Heidelberg, 1924; 26th edition in 1960).

3. K. Bednarik, *Der junge Arbeiter von heute, ein neuer Typ* (Stuttgart, 1953).

4. Helmut Schelsky, *Die skeptische Generation* (Diederichs, Düsseldorf, 1957).

5. Edgar Z. Friedenburg, *The Vanishing Adolescent* (Beacon Press, Inc., 1959; Dell Publishing Co., Inc., 1959).

6. Jean Jousselin, *Jeunesse fait social Méconnu* (Presses Universitaires, Paris, 1959).

7. J. Goudsblom, *De Nieuwe Volwassenen* (Querido, Amsterdam, 1959).

8. A remark made by Prof. Ernst Lange (of the Kirchliche Hochschule in Berlin) during a conference at the Ecumenical Institute of Bossey, Geneva, 1960.

9. Peter L. Berger, *The Noise of Solemn Assemblies* (Doubleday & Company, Inc., 1961) and *The Precarious Vision* (Doubleday & Company, Inc., 1961).

X

IS THE CHURCH IN THE WAY
OF ITS OWN RENEWAL?

THERE IS IN THE CHURCH an imminent rift between two groups, groups that are hard to define. It is not a matter of an antipathy between generations, although one of the groups seems to have more young people while the other has a majority of older people. Nor is it a matter of a dispute between institutionalists and "movement" people; in both groups Christians from inside and outside the church stand side by side. All the old distinctions we make in the church certainly have something to do with it, but they do not exactly describe the matter itself: liberal/orthodox; high church/low church; old/young; fellow travelers/haters of Communism. Neither do the theological categories fit—ontology/functionalism, Faith and Order/Life and Work, or whatever else they may be called. It is not merely a clash between intellectuals and non-academics—even this modern class distinction does not really do.

What is at stake is the unity of the church, which is being threatened by a new rift, a rift that has little to do with the confessions already in existence but which is threatening the Roman Catholic Church as much as the Pentecostal community. Or in other—and perhaps better —words it is a question of a particular rediscovery of unity in Christ, which is so strong that it not only creates a new ecumenical confession but almost a new church. And that is not to be dismissed lightly.

Until recently new denominations came into existence because, in a particular confession, a movement of renewal got started that made continued fellowship with the brethren of the same confession impossible. Lutherans, Congregationalists, Mennonites, Baptists, Methodists, Salvation Army, became separate denominations in that way.

But now something different is happening. Now a Baptist preacher is reading a book by the Catholic, Gustav Weigel, and discovers that he has more in common with this priest than with most of his Baptist colleagues. Or a good Reformed church elder reads a little book by an Anglican bishop and discovers—*horribile dictu*—that here he is faced with an authority that his own minister does not have!

Now, these are only harmless examples, but the matter becomes more delicate when a young Protestant minister in Spain, whose church has been closed by the authorities and who—because of Spain's discriminating laws—had difficulty getting legally married, discovers that in all honesty he is living in a deeper fellowship with the church renewers of Catholic Action and the revolutionary priests from the Basque country than with the evangelical colleagues in his own presbytery. And that is not an isolated example, but only one occurrence among many. Hundreds of evangelical students in South America have made this discovery and, to the horror of their parents, they have drawn their conclusions from it.

Before the "ecumaniac" rubs his hands and says, "That is great and wonderful," let us look at yet another example. In England there were a number of young Methodist ministers who at one time rumored it around that if the conversations between the Church of England and their own church collapsed, they would become Anglicans. I spent a few days with some of them and listened to old, wise (really wise) Methodists express their lack of comprehension of such an attitude. "That is no solution! Think of the theological questions. How do you stand regarding the apostolic succession? Think of the great inheritance of Methodism—its freedom, the lay preachers, the ordination of women, the lay celebration of the Communion . . ." My friends said nothing. The old Methodist (who only happened to be "old") received no answer, but also did not receive his due. And it seems to me to be of great importance not to ignore this silence but to undertake an examination of it. But no, that again is wrong. There is nothing to be examined—it can only be clarified, put in context, and understood, because with these people whom I have in mind it was far more a question of a feeling (*Lebensgefühl*) than of a theological position.

But this feeling is a position which is in the process of working itself out through our practical theology and churches. The lack of understanding shown by "the others" arises from the traditional but questionable conviction that the theological differences which we have are in fact determined by and connected with existential decisions and positions. It is beyond the comprehension of "the others" that a book could be theologically weak and at the same time pastorally strong, or that it can be a strange mixture of various—and even mutually exclusive —theologies and yet retain an indisputable authority. In the discussion with the Bishop of Woolwich, for instance, most of his admirers were immediately ready to attack every conclusion of the author; however, that does not affect the existential authority of the book. Yes, in fear and trembling I will go yet a step farther: it even increases the book's authority. This doubtful assertion deserves an explanation. And it seems possible to me that there is such an explanation.

The central words that have dominated ecumenical thinking in Europe since 1945 are: the renewal of the church. Around these words others such as secularization, unity, apostolate, experiment, and service group themselves together. This school of renewal has its apostles and teachers—people such as Kraemer, Visser 't Hooft, Wendland, Wickham, Casalis, Hoekendijk, Southcott, Küng, Congar, Symanowski, Bonhoeffer, Ebeling, Weber, MacLeod. Anyone who examines his bookshelves to find the best read books published after the war discovers these names (and those of their pupils) on the covers. Taken together they do not represent one confessional position. On the contrary! They do not belong to the same school of theology. But with all the differences, these books show up characteristics that hold these people together. And what that means can be made clear in two simple sentences. All the authors mentioned are fascinated by the completely new image of the world, and all of them have said the same thing—that the required renewal must necessarily be a *total* renewal, a renewal of life and thought.

The new world picture is presented to us with various key words—secularized, come of age, technological, industrialized, urbanized, post-Christian, differentiated. In the understanding of our society, the renewal theologians have found one another. Most of them have in fact written theological essays, studies in which the reader is challenged to think about how the church or how the Christian can live in this situation with the gospel. Their systematic theological production can often only be termed small. They were and are too fascinated by the pace of the development of history to go on sitting in their studies and writing volumes of prolegomena. What came and is coming out of their hands are hastily written analyses and "roadsigns": We must go farther in this direction. And on all the signposts is written, Total Renewal: something like the way in which an orange-colored shield with the name "Amsterdam" on all the signposts in Holland provides an almost eschatological dimension for the indicated direction to the next village. I know very well that I am asserting nothing new, but nevertheless I repeat it again for safety's sake, for example, in the words of Provost Ernest Southcott: Renewal of the church does not mean the renewal of its wallpaper but of its walls. And Woolwich writes: "One thing is pretty clear to me, namely, that my little book may appear to go astray because it is not radical enough." All the authors mentioned above finish their articles and publications with an unusually strong plea for the renewal of the life of the church, a renewal that is not a restoration, but an event in which death and resurrection are involved. As the churches said in Evanston (2d Assembly of the World Council of Churches), in those never sufficiently repeated words: The ecumenical movement is an obedience unto death.

The teachers of renewal theology have created a new school, not in a systematic but in a personal sense; they have created a school of younger and older theologians, of nontheologians, intellectuals, and nonintellectuals together. Their school must be clearly distinguished from their *public*. Their public is as large as the church. They are quoted at suitable and unsuitable times, and their books stand as high on the popularity list in the bookshops as in the presbytery or synod meetings. Their public recognizes the truth in analysis and argument but does not take them seriously. The total renewal that our renewal theologians are demanding is not forthcoming. The renewers and their followers cannot get away from the impression that the churches are continually trying to integrate renewal into the already existing structures, and to make it a partial, restrained operation. The churches are ready to remodel the old house to a certain extent, to paint it up, and if necessary, even to make some alterations, but the total renewal, the beginning again from scratch—this is not happening. The real battle has not yet started.

Even after the violent reaction against John Robinson, things have become quiet again. The churches are biding their time, and even write appreciative critiques about all these new ideas in their church magazines. It keeps things going. And, the public knows, postponement is the best road to complacency. The friendly murder of apostles of renewal has lasted since the war. And some of them have fallen. It would be too painful to go into personal details here, but anyone who knows one or more of the people mentioned knows what happened—the embittered men and the men who have laid down their weapons are legion. Does all this mean that the above is nothing more than a group of weak voices crying in the wilderness? Is the renewal of the church a bee in the bonnet that can easily be replaced by another? In the eternal battle between institutionalism and movement in the church, has the former won? I don't believe so. The existing experiments contradict such a conclusion, experiments that in fact are in motion and remain living (statisticians may stay quietly at home—the figures are hardly significant). In every land and in every church the discovery is being made that a total renewal *is* taking place in small groups, often unnoticed, often making no impression for a while—but it is happening.

I hesitate again to name people. How many experiments have already been petrified too early because the public worshiped as a solution what was intended to serve as no more than an indication? I know three or four house churches in Eastern Europe in which total renewal is being experienced. Likewise, there have been parishes in France in which no clericalism rules; there has also been some youth work in Holland which is an example of the missionary structure of the churches. These few experiments are there, and they comprise the salt of our existence. However, the renewal theologians have done more. They have not only pleasantly entertained a large public and set up a few teachers. Those are the ones who could be described as the "no answer yet" people. That may sound somewhat theatrical, but the truth is hard enough. Alex Vidler once said that we can best serve the cause of truth and the church—this we willingly admit—where our confusions are to be found and not by bringing forward all sorts of statements. For the theologians are, as far as we can see, not in a position today which could justify such a thing. This simple comment does not merely say that there is little new material to bring forward. It is also a concrete critique of what was asserted with such certainty earlier.

It often seems to me that the renewal school does not have so much difficulty with the reality of today as with the heritage of yesterday. The church is the problem, and not society. Society (the world) is rediscovered in renewal theology as a laboratory of God, in which he carries out his experiments. Pagans are the bearers of the promise, and within the circle of the renewers there are open eyes and open ears for what Christ says to them through the world. "What I know of the church," says J. M. somewhere in Eastern Europe, "the Communists have taught me. They have broken down the unreality which the church has upheld, and given back to us the essential things of being the church." "When our experiment (house church) came into being," tells P. S., "the world came to wish us luck and to express the wish to be allowed to take part, but the church has from the beginning tried to destroy the whole thing." And Edgar Friedenberg once remarked in a lecture in New York that the church knows everything. It knows God and the Bible. It knows how, when, and why Jesus died, rose, and ascended into heaven. It knows also—happily—that now it must be renewed, and its failure in a new society has quickly been written up in little books and so has become nice and respectable.

The renewal school has read so well what the modern theologians—welcomed by the church—have said that it has also gradually come to believe it. Perhaps first of all everything must be razed to the ground so that something new may be built up from the rubbish. An older colleague said to me recently: "You get things clear as soon as there is a dispute somewhere in the church." The remark referred to the *Honest to God* debate. And he was right. Wherever there is a dispute, there it would be possible for complete renewal to set in. And once again, *total* renewal is what the postwar theologians demanded and what the church accepted as "canonical." Suspicion toward the church, often also despair about the church, does not stem from the spirit of our time, but is a direct result of the discrepancy between the renewal theology that was welcomed joyfully by the churches and the restoration work that is in fact taking place. The suspicion toward the church has to be seen in the context of a new fascination with the gospel.

A student friend visited us not long ago and said: "I have seriously tried to make Kraemer's *A Theology of the Laity*[1] and Margull's *Hope in Action*[2] the basis of my work in my parish. But it doesn't work! The structures of my parish are such that these things cannot be introduced into the framework of today. Therefore, I do not even dare to start on industry apostles like Wendland, Wickham, and Symanowski."

This remark is characteristic. For both Kraemer and Margull have from the beginning drawn attention to the fact that the renewal of the church is a total matter—pertaining to both structure and content—and cannot be glued onto old structures. But the church—professors and leading preachers—had given him the impression that the combination was indeed possible. And when he saw that this was not the case, he gave it up.

In Union Theological Seminary in New York, Theodore

Wedel says it is the fashion for young theologians not to want to go into parish work. A large percentage of the candidates who have completed their studies choose other vocations or disappear into the thousands of possibilities for extraparochial work in the American churches. This is a related phenomenon. I get a bit annoyed with the word "fashion" in Wedel's remark, because in my opinion the same crisis bears its prints here: the renewal theology will not let itself be built into old church structures, and those who accept it do not know what to do with it in their existing church structures.

And so a new group of people asserts itself in the church, who congregate theologically around the renewal theology, but see only a few possibilities to work out practically what they have recognized as being true. In the ecumenical movement of today they play a strange role. I do not think I exaggerate if I say that they are not actually playing a role in the machinery of the confessional discussion. Although theologically able to participate, they do not feel themselves at home there. Systematics and most priorities of "Faith and Order" are offensive to them. Perhaps we should even say that they no longer have any interest in the formal ecumenical movement as such. We must be careful here—they are not confessionalists who raise their own church above the others. Quite the opposite. But the division of the church into denominations seems to them actually unimportant. They feel the separation between renewers and restorers in all churches to be much more important than the ever-recurring theological disputes on historical divisions. A good example of this is to be found in England in the conversations between Anglicans and Methodists. The Faith and Order questions in this discussion are about the ministry, the Sacraments, and the relation between church and state. Among the renewers there exists scarcely any interest in these questions, but with them it is a matter of the reunion of the renewal potential, the common apostolate to industry, the request for a new structure, etc. Nobody denies that the first triad hangs together with the second, but what is decisive is what is chosen as priority and from which angle the work of reunion is approached.

And the old guards in the *oikoumene* should not now think that we are dealing here with the old discussion between "Faith and Order" and "Life and Work," for the interesting thing about the development is exactly this: that the renewers regard the questions of Life and Work as Faith and Order priorities. It seems to me that here the essential integration of Faith and Order and Life and Work is being shown. It is, therefore, no wonder that the study on the missionary structure of the congregation is one of the most popular undertakings of the World Council of Churches at the moment.

The contribution of the renewers to the ecumenical movement often seems small and marginal. It should not surprise us that their activities and writings appear more as *ad hoc* explosions than as continuous contributions. The institution of the ecumenical movement can only bring them together against the often heard reproach of the churches, that "these people are a fringe group in their own church who don't represent anything." In their own confessions the renewers lead a strange existence as well. Their own church fellowship is certainly not their spiritual home. Their community is much wider, but also much less tangible. Denominations are, in their eyes, a necessary evil, because they know that the church has to be a visible entity. Their role within the denomination is necessarily a critical one. They live in it under protest. They rebel against the dogged complacency with which the churches regard themselves. The present structure of the local parishes and of the whole church is always experienced from the perspective of the renewal theology and therefore can't stand up. Therefore, the renewers are often also bad churchgoers. Sunday morning is for them a torture. And this is not because of pride but of despair.

"To go to church on Sunday morning," one of them was reported to have said, "is for me an experience like that of the kitchen chef of Louis XIV, who had to eat dry bread in the Bastille." But most do go all the same. Why? Usually for the sake of the visible church, of the sense of fellowship, and of the mystery. But not out of loyalty and thankfulness for what they receive, or from custom.

The crisis of renewal theology does not leave the personal, spiritual life untouched. One of the most striking reactions to John Robinson's *Honest to God* is that of relief: a bishop who has difficulty with his prayer life! The forms of our life of faith—Bible-reading, telling of Bible stories to our children, and prayer life—are questioned a good deal today. The problems of communication between the renewers and the others are very much connected with the existential spiritual poverty the individual has to live with today. The despair about the church is linked with the discovery that I by myself can do absolutely nothing. The Christian community is essential for the survival of the believer. And again we recognize one of the ever-recurring themes of renewal theology. Christianity is a community matter and not an individual affair. But that only becomes clear when the individual discovers that he by himself cannot expect growth in his spiritual life. For many, the only spiritual experience that functions is essentially linked with an experience in the group. When the group experience falls away, everything falls away. But the church is still built on what Riesman calls the "inner-directed" person, the individualist, who experiences the reality of his faith alone and—so strengthened—carries out his contribution to the community. The inner-directed believer does not know the despairing feeling of the spiritual void, a silent God, and the breakdown of a personal morality. And even if he does know this, he can cope with it because of his personal and sufficient resources.

The dividing line in the church runs, then, between those who experience doubt as something creative, and those who look at doubt as a form of unbelief. The "doubting dons" of Oxford and Cambridge have brought about a division. One group draws its breath relieved: "How good to find men who really take the courage to start again! At last, leaders who have recognized that nothing can be taken for granted!" The other group raises its eyebrows without understanding: Does nothing remain? The one group says, "Let us share the confusion of the congregation," whereas the other is afraid of confusing the laity.

Above all, the repeated observation that the old morality has lost its legitimacy fills them with fear. A few years ago, in a serious theological article in England, connection was made between the Profumo affair and the new morality theologians from the Quakers to Woolwich—a brilliant example of how panic-stricken the reaction is.

I hope the argument is clear: A large group of theologians, and not seldom the keenest observers, develop a new feeling for life (*Lebensgefühl*) in response to a renewal theory, which is well-known in the churches, but not followed by them. Because of this feeling-for-life they often do not feel themselves in a position to take part in the traditional discussions. They keep themselves rather apart in the ecumenical movement and are *enfants terribles* in their own denomination. They find their teachers among the critics and demolishers rather than among the systematicians in the theological world. To them the exception is often more real than the rule, and the experiment more real than the regular order of things. In the theological discussion with "the others" they cut a bad figure, because they cannot handle the systematic-theological concepts without losing their integrity. They are bad churchgoers and often silent sheep. The group has members among pastors, professors, and the laity.

What should we say to this? Two things would be disastrous—to ignore and to integrate. If the group were ignored, they might begin to build their own structure or to disappear, and in both cases they would be lost to the church. But to integrate them is even more dangerous. If people from the group I have described were now called to high posts in the existing structure, they might have to give up their demand for total renewal. There are many who are integrated into the structure and have paid the price—wild geese who have been tamed. But what then? There remains but one thing: for the church to learn how essential is the experiment in their midst, and give money, room, and freedom to the renewers to try out and to formulate the vision of the renewal of the church. It may well be that it will be scornfully noted that the "old structures" must after all pay for all these experiments. I have never understood what is wrong with that. If the traditional structures are no longer willing to help pay for new structures and experimental ministries, they have become conservative. The renewal of the church is not an attempt to form another denomination! Renewal is no goal in itself, but is happening for the benefit of the whole church so that the whole church should be a worthy witness to the gospel. If the church (and I write intentionally in the singular) were to take seriously the necessity of its renewal, it would permanently bring together the younger renewers and would force them to work out their experiments practically.

NOTES

1. Hendrik Kraemer, *A Theology of the Laity* (Lutterworth Press, London, 1958; The Westminster Press, 1958).
2. Hans J. Margull, *Hope in Action* (Muhlenberg Press, 1962).